the KODAK Workshop Series

Using Your Automatic/Autofocus Camera

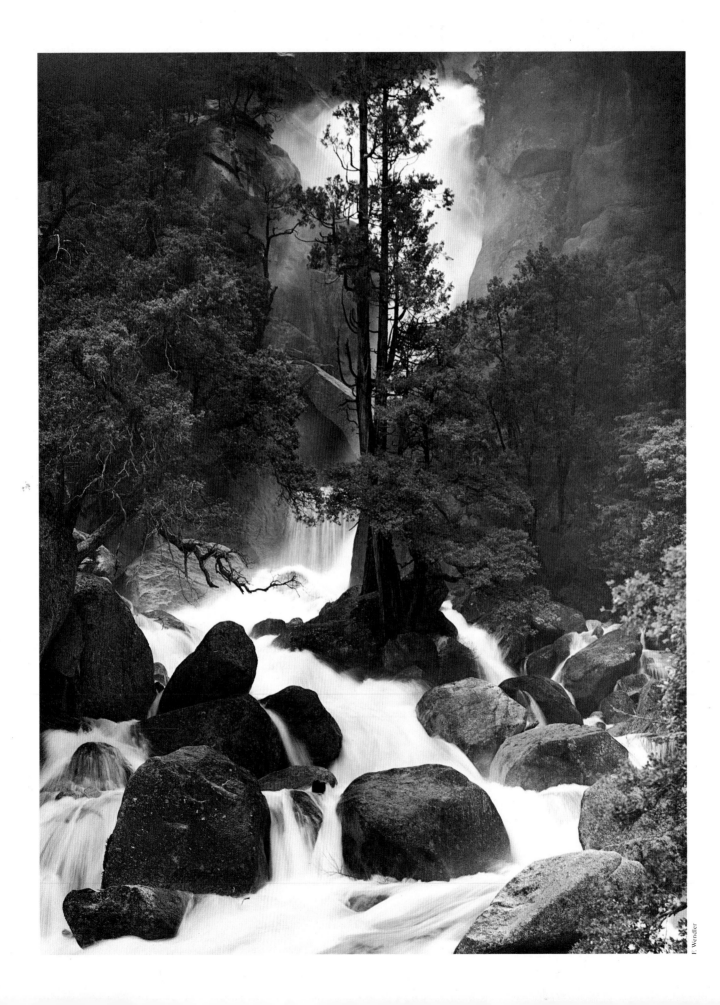

Using Your Automatic/Autofocus Camera

by the editors of Eastman Kodak Company

the KODAK Workshop Series
Helping to expand your understanding of photography

Using Your Automatic/Autofocus Camera
By the editors of Eastman Kodak Company

Kodak Editor: Derek Doeffinger

Original design by Roger Pring
Revised layout by Dan Malczewski

Equipment photography by Tom Beelmann and
Michelle Hallen Infantino

Cover photograph by André Chastel

Picture research by William Paris

Photographic Products Group
Eastman Kodak Company
Rochester, NY 14650

KODAK Publication KW-11
CAT 143 9603
Library of Congress Catalog Card Number 81-67431
ISBN 0-87985-368-9

3-86 BX Major Revision
Printed in the United States of America

*Throughout this book Kodak products are recommended.
Other materials may be used, but equivalent results
might not be obtained.*

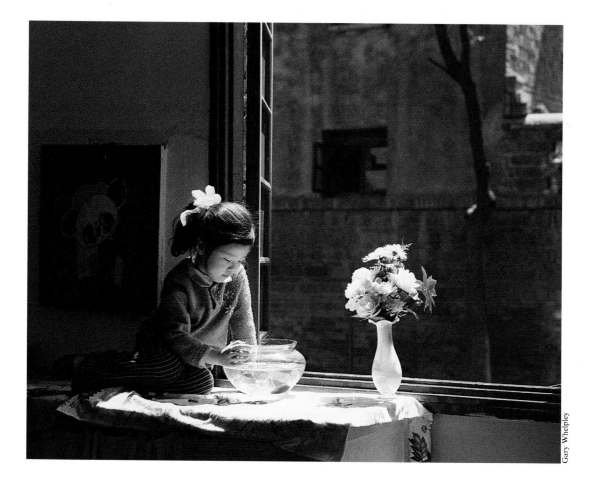

Introduction

Like many other devices, automatic cameras have been riding that tide of technological innovation known as the electronic chip. It's a heady tide that has excited many in the field of photography. One camera design engineer has even proclaimed that he builds personal computers that take pictures. And each week at the newsstand, photography magazines herald the newest automatic camera and reveal how it will simplify photography. But no one should be more excited about automatic cameras than the photographer. For automation has proven to be a boon for snapshooters and professionals alike.

Only a few years ago some photographers thought buying an automatic camera a risky proposition. They didn't relish relinquishing control to electromechanical devices they didn't understand. Today, most people still don't understand how the automation works, but they want automatic cameras because they know they do work.

Exactly what is an automatic camera? Originally, it was a camera that set its own shutter or lens aperture or both to produce a correctly exposed picture. In other words, it wasn't all that automatic. However, today's automatic cameras offer more than just automatic exposure. Automatic focusing, automatic film advance and rewind, automatic film-speed setting, and automatic built-in flash are also commonly found on cameras.

The most basic automatic cameras are point-and-shoot machines that require little more of the photographer than pushing a button. That's simple. If your photographic needs are limited, these cameras will serve you well.

More complex and challenging photographic pursuits, however, require more complex and versatile cameras. In addition to pushing a button, you must also set or monitor the shutter speed and lens aperture, and consider how they will affect the picture. That's not so simple. Fortunately, the actual operation of even

complex cameras is fairly easy. Whether your camera is complex or simple, study your camera manual and carry it with you until you're confident operating your camera.

In this book we'll introduce you to the different types of automatic cameras and accessories, such as zoom lenses and electronic flashes. We'll study the camera controls and show you how to use them to improve your pictures. We'll also take a long look at the essence of automatic cameras—automatic exposure. Automatic exposure isn't perfect, so you need to know when to override your camera's exposure setting and how to get the right exposure.

Since the purpose of automation is to free you to concentrate on the subject, we'll develop your awareness of light, color, composition, and other elements important in revealing the subject. If you have a favorite subject, such as people, landscapes, or action, you'll find specific tips and techniques for better picture-taking.

Contents

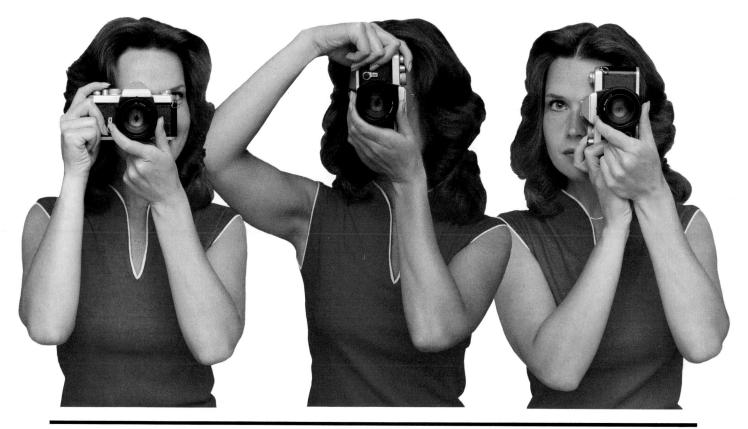

Hold the camera against your face in a relaxed but firm grip. Don't hold it so tightly that your muscles become tense. Tuck your arms along your sides. Grasp the lens so you can focus without changing your grip.

*For vertical pictures, you can position the camera with the shutter release on top of the camera, **middle**, or on the bottom, **right**. Choose the position more comfortable.*

Wait until you are holding the camera steadily before you press the shutter button. Then gently increase pressure on the shutter button until it trips. Do not jab at the shutter or you will jar the camera, causing blurred pictures.

First

HOLD THE CAMERA STEADY AND LEVEL
So complete is the electronic wizardry of modern cameras that their manufacturers boast that you need only push a button—the camera will do the rest. That motto is almost but not quite true. In addition to selecting and composing a scene, you not only have to hold the camera, you have to hold it steady and level.

Holding the camera steady and level is the most basic of basics and would seem to be well within the capabilities of most of us. And 95 percent of the time it is. But like the runner who trips just before crossing the finish line, it is a basic that if not observed can cost you dearly with blurred or crooked pictures.

If your camera allows you to set the shutter speed, use a fast shutter speed to prevent picture blur caused by camera movement. For most picture-taking with the normal camera lens (50 mm lens), make it a practice to use a shutter speed of 1/125 second or faster. When necessary, you can obtain sharp pictures at slower shutter speeds if you have extra steady hands or if you brace yourself against a tree, column, or railing. For other lenses, use a shutter speed that is approximately 2X the focal length of the lens. For instance, with a 135 mm lens, choose a shutter speed of 1/250 second. For a 250 mm lens, choose a shutter speed of 1/500 second. If need be, you can use a shutter speed roughly equal to the lens' focal length. Example: 1/125 second for a 135 mm lens.

Set in a program mode (see p. 32), some cameras automatically provide a shutter speed fast enough to offset slight camera movement. But in dim light, even they will be forced to set a slower shutter speed. Always monitor your automatic camera to be sure it is providing a fast enough shutter speed. If it isn't, take over and set your own shutter speed or gain additional support if forced to use a slow shutter speed.

PHOTO TIPS

All the whiz-bang electronics of automatic cameras help you only to achieve pictures that are better technically. They do nothing to improve the art of the photograph, the seeing of the photograph. That's where you must take over. The tips that follow will help you do that. But remember, they're just tips. They'll work in many but not all situations. But if you use some of them, thoughtfully choose not to use others, but ever think about how to photograph the scene before you, then more and more you'll find yourself making photographs that appeal not only to you but to others, too.

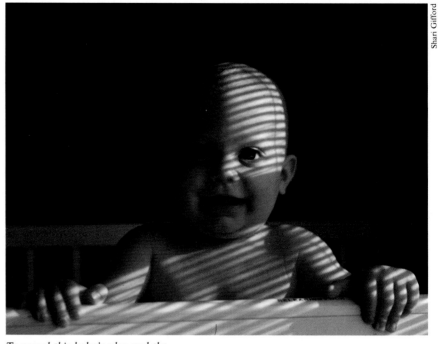

To reveal this baby's glee and the shadow pattern made by the blind, the photographer moved in close so the baby would fill the picture area and become the inescapable subject.

Get Close (see page 74)

The one piece of advice that accompanies all advice about improving photos is "Get close." Just as the eye ignores distracting surroundings so does its concentrate on a subject so intently that the subject seems to dominate and appear larger than it actually is. In reality, it often fills but a fraction of the picture area. The only way to be sure that you are emphasizing the subject is to make it large in the picture. Either physically move in close or do it optically by using a telephoto lens. In general have the main subject fill half or more of the picture area.

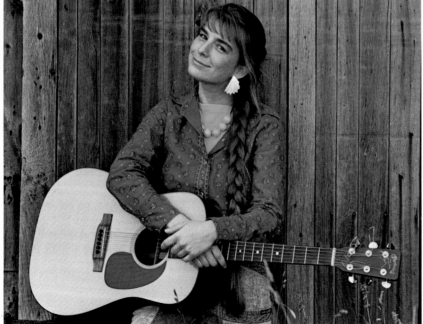

Because a plain, non-competing background was used, this young lady's bemused expression and twinkling eyes exert their full charm.

Simplify (see page 74)

When you view something to photograph, your mind tends to focus on this subject exclusively, filtering out the surroundings. But the camera catches all that is before you, and as many a photo has proven, there is a great deal before you other than the subject. So simplify. Find a viewpoint that yields a plain background. Move in close; use a telephoto lens. By simplifying, you show the subject clearly so there's no doubt it is the subject.

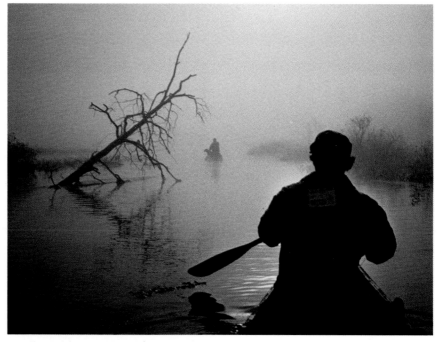

Compose with care (see page 72)

Composition is the arrangement of subjects within a photograph to give proper emphasis and a pleasing appearance. Although any composition that works can be considered good, the following guidelines will often improve a photo.

1. Place the subject off-center.

2. Use strong lines and shapes.

3. Choose a viewpoint to emphasize the main subject.

4. Ignore these tips for any compelling composition.

5. Take extra pictures, varying composition.

By placing the canoeist in the foreground, by having him emerge from the bottom of the frame, and by freezing the paddle just as it is about to slice into the water, the photographer created a sense of immediacy and reality that makes the viewer feel as if he or she is sitting in the stern.

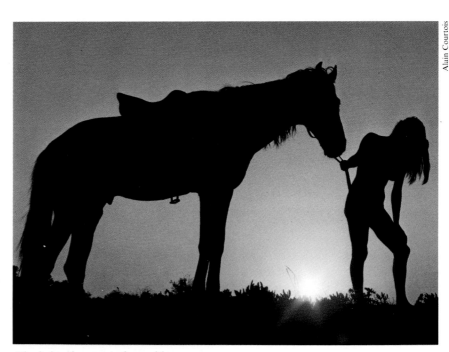

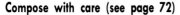

Watch the light (see page 61)

Most amateur photographers think subject matter is the most important part of a photograph. They look for majestic mountains, dramatic bluffs, and smiling faces. Although professional photographers realize the importance of subject matter, they know the lighting of the subject often determines the success of the photograph. Light can be bland and dull (as it often is at midday). But it can also be soft and sensuous, bold and dramatic. Become aware of light on a subject (your own house) at different times of day, from different angles, in different weather and seasons. As you learn to use light, your photos will begin to show the professional touch.

The light of sunset is favored by many photographers. The technique for making a silhouette is explained on page 75.

Dramatize by viewpoint (see page 76)

Far and away most of our pictures are taken looking straight ahead from a position about 5½ feet above the ground—a viewpoint that can become boring through sheer repetition. Vary your viewpoint. Occasionally kneel or lay on the ground and shoot looking up or straight ahead; from a low viewpoint, tulips and daffodils can seem as tall as poplars and oaks. Try a high viewpoint, and see the new shapes and patterns that emerge— from an airplane the fields below begin to look like a giant quilt.

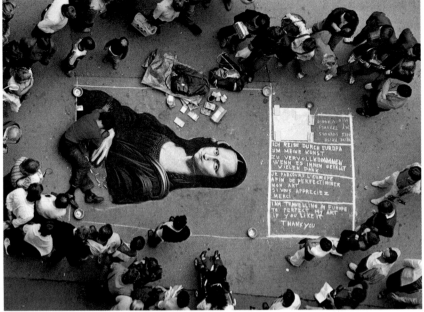

Only a high viewpoint can reveal this sidewalk artist at work and his goals spelled out in three languages on the right side of the picture.

Arouse feelings

Photographs that make the viewer respond, be it a laugh or a smile, a gasp or a sigh, a frown or a smirk, are photos that work. One obvious ploy is to record the lively spirits of others— children frolicking, grandmother pensively peering out the window. Less obvious is to rely on the power of association. A park bench, unoccupied and covered with snow, may reflect loneliness. A single ocean wave breaking onto the beach might represent freedom. Photographs that succeed in capturing your feelings about a scene will relay those feelings to the viewer.

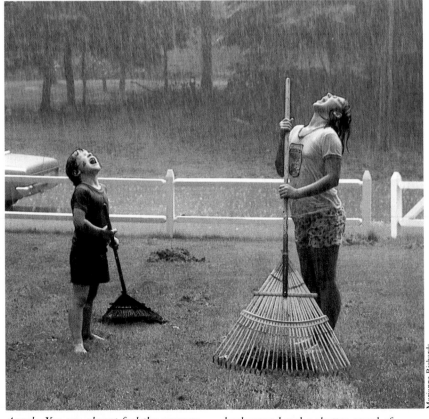

Aaaah. You can almost feel the summer downpour splashing on your face and trickling down your neck. The joy in this picture is irresistible. A dark-toned background and a shutter speed of roughly 1/60 second were used to reveal the rain as streaks.

Show people doing something

Time-honored though they may be, those old standby's, "Say cheese" and "Look at the birdy" are two worn-out phrases that can produce worn-out pictures. Sure it's nice to have a picture of Aunt Hortense and Uncle Horace with big smiles, but how about a few pictures that reveal their personality—Hortense hefting a sack of fertilizer destined for the garden or Horace filling the bird feeder. Showing people in action not only describes them but injects story-telling drama into the picture.

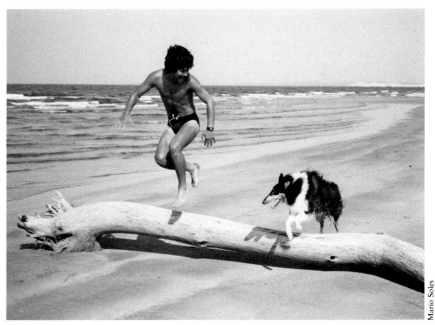

Running along the beach with one's dog is a simple activity that invigorates this photograph.

Take extra pictures

Another important difference between a professional and amateur photographer is that a pro often shoots many rolls of film of a single subject using a variety of angles and compositions. And from those many rolls, he hopes to find the one or two photos that catch the elusive essence of the subject. It's impractical and expensive for you to shoot many rolls. But when you hope to catch the whimsical expression of your daughter cuddling her cat or the fading light spilling across the Grand Canyon, when you hope to catch the essence of a subject, you, too, should take many pictures. That's the best way to increase your chances of success.

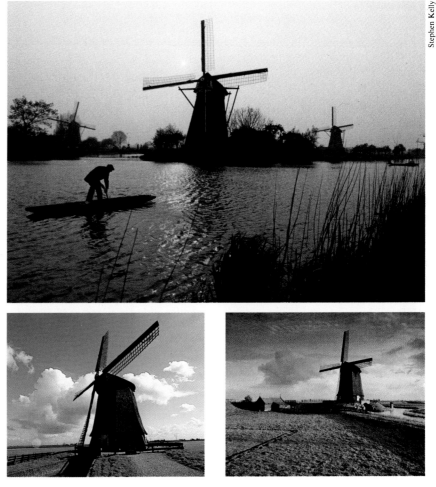

Often the best angle and composition for a photograph evolves after an exploration of the many possibilities.

11

Automatic cameras

There is a great variety of automatic cameras: disc cameras, 110 cameras, 6 x 4.5 cameras, 6 x 7 cameras, $2^{1}/_{4}$ cameras, and, of course, the most popular of all, the 35 mm cameras. Although automatic cameras come in a lot of sizes, shapes, and forms, and vary greatly in their sophistication, they all share a basic form that harks back to the first camera that ever made a photograph. Each is a lighttight box. At the back of the box is a piece of film. At the front of the box is a lens. The lens projects an image of the scene onto the film. The film records the image.

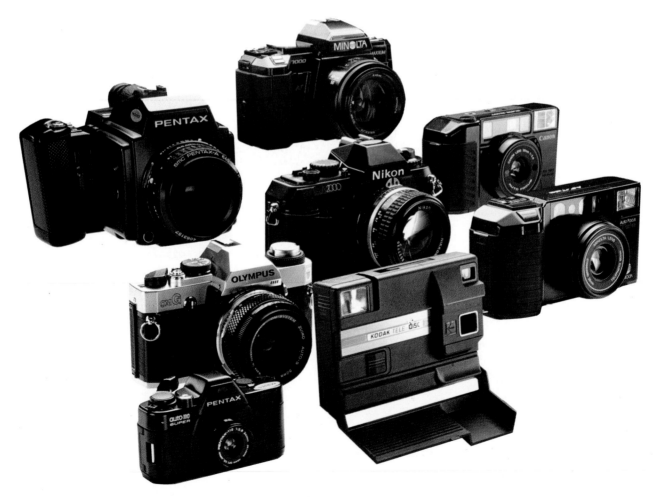

35 mm CAMERAS

The 35 mm camera is the most popular camera format. The reasons are threefold: The film is big enough to yield superior prints yet small enough to fit into a compact camera; many types of films are made for 35 mm cameras; the cameras themselves, especially SLR cameras, are quite versatile and easy to use.

The two basic types of 35 mm cameras are single-lens-reflex (SLR) cameras and compact cameras. The latest SLR cameras include nearly all the automatic features of compact autofocus cameras, such as automatic film advance and rewind, and automatic focusing.

Each camera type can take outstanding pictures. The main difference between them is that the SLR camera is the center of a system of lenses, flashes, and other accessories that you can use to further your photographic endeavors. Compact cameras are designed for more casual photography—although in the hands of a serious photographer they are not to be underestimated.

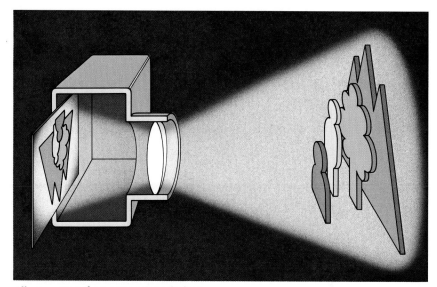

All conventional cameras are variations on the basic theme shown here: a lighttight chamber with a lens at one end and a piece of film at the other.

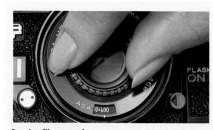

Set the film speed
If your camera doesn't automatically set film speed, be sure that you do each time you load film. If your camera back has a memo holder, stick the flap from the film carton in it so you can later double check the film speed setting.

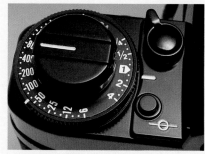

Set the compensation control at neutral
Before taking pictures, verify that the compensation control is set to give normal exposure. Some compensation controls are atop the ISO dial, making it possible to accidentally misset either control.

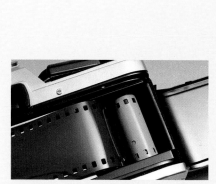

Loading film into a 35 mm camera
A short strip of film called a leader extends from a 35 mm magazine. Unless you have automatic film loading, you must slip the leader into the slotted take-up spool. Before closing the camera back, advance the film with the film advance lever until the toothed drive wheels engage both the top and bottoms rows of perforations. Now close the camera back. Advance the film until the frame counter shows you are ready to take the first picture.

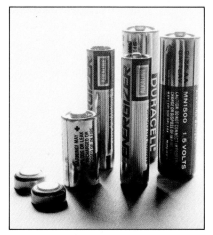

Without batteries many automatic cameras don't function or function at only one shutter speed and leave you to guess the correct exposure. Regularly check the camera's batteries and always keep a spare set with you.

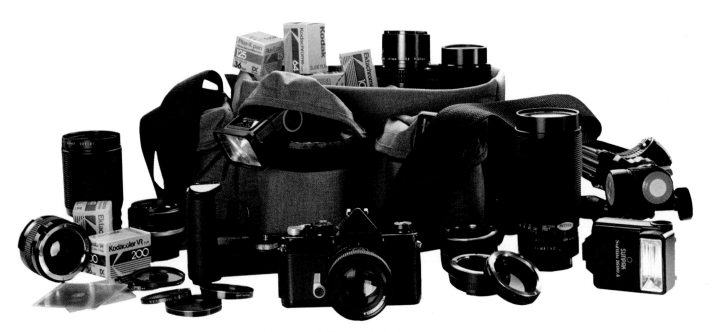

An automatic 35 mm single-lens reflex (SLR) camera can cope with complex photographic situations through a wide range of available accessories.

35 mm SLR Cameras

Versatility and control. That's the theme of 35 mm SLR cameras. Through camera controls or accessories, you can manipulate the scene before you to alter or preserve its appearance. You can interpret. Or you can document.

For instance, by setting a slow shutter speed you can transform a galloping thoroughbred into a flowing ribbon resplendent with grace and beauty; by using a fast shutter speed you can sculpt every muscle fiber to reveal power and strength. By choosing a small lens opening (aperture), you can sharply reveal a gardener and her prize roses in the background; by setting a large opening you can blur the flowers into a colorful background that sets off the sharp portrait of the gardener. And working together, a large aperture and a slow shutter speed can let you take pictures in the dim light of a wine cellar or a Parisian bistro. Many of the feats achieved by adjusting aperture and shutter speed

(more on p. 22) are not possible with simpler, nonadjustable cameras.

By far the SLR's versatility stems from the number of accessories it can use. Wide-angle lenses, telephoto lenses, flash units, macro and zoom lenses, tripods, a variety of filters, data backs, interchangeable viewfinder screens, and underwater housings form a fraction of the accessories available. An SLR camera is the foundation on which to build a photographic system. With accessories you can specialize. A macro lens enables you to take excellent close-up photos of butterflies and flowers. A 300 mm telephoto lens enables you to photograph your daughter kicking the winning soccer goal. A tripod and slow shutter speed permit you to make a time exposure that captures the bloom of color at a fireworks display.

In short, the capability to adjust camera controls or use accessories extends your photographic skills and

the excellence of your pictures. If you truly like to take pictures, a 35 mm SLR camera is the one for you.

Single-lens-reflex (SLR) cameras are so named because a single lens forms the image that you view and the image that the film records. The viewfinder is directly behind and above the lens. A mirror and prism intercept light passing through the lens and divert it to the viewfinder to form the image you see. In single-lens-reflex camera, the word reflex means an image formed by reflection. The trademark of SLR cameras is that you see the same scene the film sees.

At the moment of picture-taking, the mirror flips up and out of the way; the shutter opens, and the image formed by the lens strikes the film to make a picture. The shutter closes, and the mirror returns to its viewing position, again reflecting the image up to the viewfinder. All that happens in an instant.

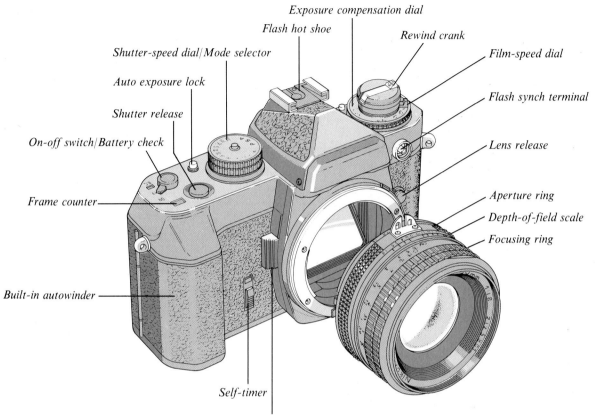

Exposure compensation dial

Flash hot shoe

Rewind crank

Shutter-speed dial/Mode selector

Film-speed dial

Auto exposure lock

Flash synch terminal

Shutter release

On-off switch/Battery check

Lens release

Frame counter

Aperture ring

Depth-of-field scale

Focusing ring

Built-in autowinder

Self-timer

Depth-of-field preview lever

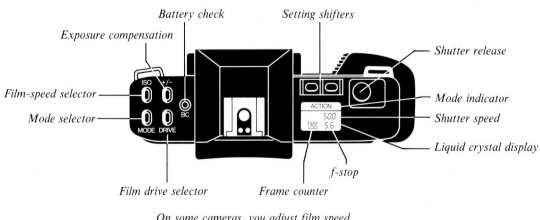

Battery check

Setting shifters

Exposure compensation

Shutter release

Film-speed selector

Mode indicator

Mode selector

Shutter speed

Liquid crystal display

Film drive selector

Frame counter

f-stop

On some cameras, you adjust film speed, aperture size, shutter speed, and exposure digitally by pressing the appropriate button.

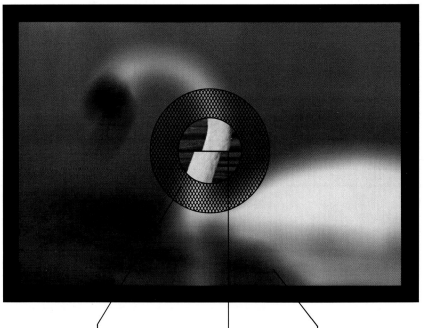

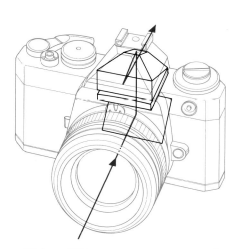

With an SLR camera, you compose and focus an image formed by the camera lens. A mirror and prism shuttle the image formed by the lens to the viewfinder where you observe it.

Split-image viewfinder

Microprism ring

Ground glass

*To help you focus, most SLR cameras have a central split-image rangefinder, a microprism around the rangefinder, and a ground glass for the rest of the area. Compare the out-of-focus image, **top**, to the in-focus image, **opposite page**.*

Focusing an SLR Camera

Conventional SLR cameras require manual focusing. While looking into the viewfinder you turn a ring on the lens until the image appears sharp. Focusing is that simple. And it's made easier by focusing aids in the viewfinder that help you distinguish an out-of-focus image from a focused one.

With autofocus SLRs, you need to center the subject in the viewfinder when taking the picture so that the autofocus system can focus on the subject (see page 19). If you don't want the subject centered, you can lock in the focus with the subject centered, then reframe the scene; or on some cameras, you can switch to manual focus. Autofocus SLRs use a passive focusing system that compares two separate images of the

scene to determine sharp focus. The autofocus system may not work well in dim light or in scenes with low contrast (such as a solid-colored blanket in shade). The viewfinder of an autofocus SLR usually provides indicators for focus confirmation, subject too close, contrast too low, and the direction to turn the lens when in manual focus.

With both manual focus and autofocus SLRs, the scene you see in the viewfinder is provided by the lens' largest aperture (typically $f/1.8$ or $f/2$), which admits more light than any of the other apertures. Thus you have a bright subject image to focus on. However, if you had set the aperture ring to another setting, such as $f/8$, (or if the camera has been set to adjust the aperture automatically),

the moment you press the shutter release, the aperture narrows to that setting to make the photo. If this picture-taking aperture is smaller than the aperture used for viewing (and it usually is), more things will appear in focus in the picture than did in the viewfinder (a smaller aperture gives more front-to-back sharpness).

To judge what the actual overall sharpness will be in a picture, many cameras provide a depth-of-field preview lever. When you actuate it, the lens sets the aperture that will be used to take the picture. You can then study the image in the viewfinder to see if zone of sharpness (depth of field) is acceptable. See page 24 for more on aperture and depth of field.

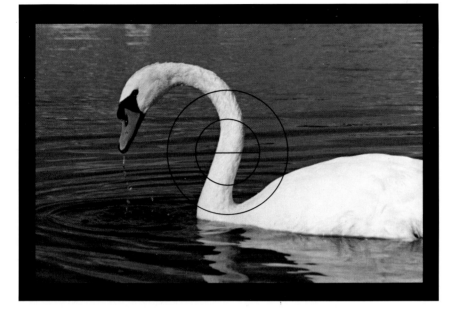

Viewfinder Information

An SLR's viewfinder does more than let you frame the scene before you. Like a bulletin board it also posts the status of camera settings. Monitoring your camera's viewfinder should become as second-nature as checking for traffic before crossing the street. Depending on the camera model, the viewfinder may indicate

- the shutter speed and aperture for correct exposure
- the automatic mode being used
- under- or overexposure
- use of too slow a shutter speed
- the need for flash
- the readiness of the flash

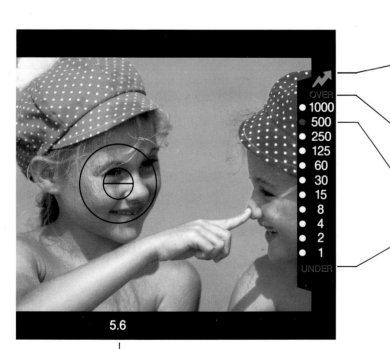

Flash symbol
1. *Blinking symbol means flash needed.*
2. *Steady lit symbol means flash charged.*
3. *After firing, green or blinking symbol indicates correct flash exposure. Red symbol indicates incorrect exposure.*

Overexposure warning

Shutter speed selected

Underexposure warning

A typical viewfinder display in an automatic 35 mm SLR shows you the lens aperture, shutter speed, and signals indicating under- or overexposure conditions. The amount of information provided and the manner of displaying it vary from model to model.

f-stop selected (Aperture)

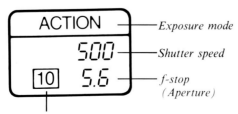

Exposure mode

Shutter speed

f-stop (Aperture)

Frame counter

Some cameras have a liquid-crystal display atop the camera that supplements viewfinder information. It may display exposure mode, f-stop and shutter speed, a frame counter, film loading, and more.

17

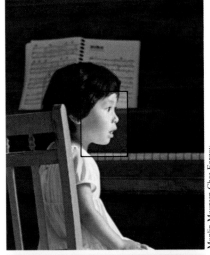

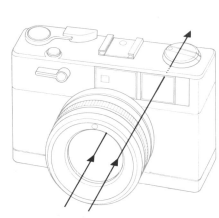

Compact 35 mm cameras have a direct vision viewfinder that functions independently from the lens. The viewfinder is a window through which you view the subject directly.

Compact 35 mm Cameras

Compact 35 mm cameras include non-SLR autofocus, fixed focus, and rangefinder cameras. With a model like the KODAK VR 35 Camera K-12, you truly need only to point and shoot, and let the camera do the rest. This autofocus camera reads DX-coded film (see p. 58) to automatically set film speed; it automatically turns on the flash and fires it, and the flash can be used for fill-flash. Used with 35 mm film, such as KODACOLOR VR-G 100, pictures will be sharp and well exposed.

In the most common type of autofocusing, the camera transmits an infrared signal toward the center of the picture field. The camera picks up the signal reflected by the subject, then calculates the distance, and focuses the lens. For accurate focusing, the subject must be centered in the viewfinder.

To focus a conventional rangefinder camera, you adjust the lens until a double image of the subject seen in the viewfinder merges into one image. Both camera types often use pictographs (a head, a full figure, mountains) in the viewfinder to indicate distance settings.

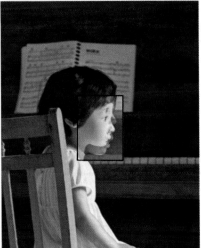

Manlin Maureen Chee Forgay

When viewing the subject through a coincidence-type optical rangefinder you see a double image when the lens is not focused on the subject. Focusing the lens merges the two images into one.

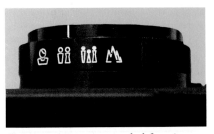

Some cameras use a symbol focusing scale to indicate close, middle, and far distances.

Cameras with fixed-focus lenses are factory set to give sharp pictures from roughly five feet to infinity. The focus cannot be adjusted by the user. The medium aperture (typically $f/5.6$) required by these cameras to assure sufficient depth of field admits less light than the larger apertures available on other cameras. Thus flash must be used more frequently with these cameras than with the other types.

Autofocus cameras are usually automatic right down to the built-in pop-up flash. Some of their rangefinder counterparts may lack some of the amenities, such as motorized film advance and built-in flash. However, some rangefinders offer manual exposure override, giving you control over shutter and aperture.

Unlike SLRs, the viewfinder of a compact camera is separate from the lens system. The viewfinder frames a slightly different area of the scene than that seen by the lens. The framing difference becomes important in close-up photos. When taking close-up pictures, use the close-up frame marks in the viewfinder. If the subject, as seen in the viewfinder, extends beyond these marks, it will be cropped off in the final picture.

If you want more than snapshooting, you need consider the disadvantages of compact cameras. They don't accept interchangeable lenses or many of the other accessories SLRs can use (although screw-on or built-in telephoto and screw-on wide-angle lenses may be available). You have little or no control over shutter speed and aperture. Shutter-speed range is often abbreviated, a typical range being from 1/15 to 1/500 second, compared with 2 seconds to 1/1000 second for an SLR. In short, you can make excellent pictures with compact cameras, but you can't achieve the creativity offered by additional controls and equipment.

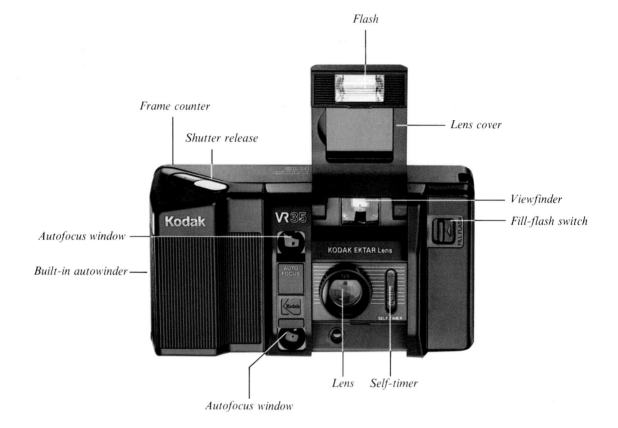

Flash

Frame counter

Shutter release

Lens cover

Viewfinder

Fill-flash switch

Autofocus window

Built-in autowinder

Autofocus window

Lens   Self-timer

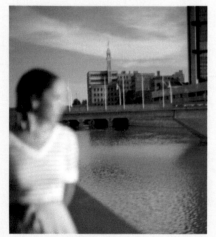

Out-of-focus

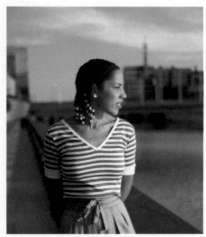

In-focus

AUTOMATIC FOCUSING

Because autofocus cameras work by determining the distance from the camera to the center of the picture area, your primary subject must be positioned in the center of the viewfinder. If your subject isn't positioned centrally, it will probably be rendered out of focus.

Many autofocus cameras have a focus lock that enables you to take sharp pictures of subjects positioned off-center. You use it by positioning your subject centrally and locking in the focus with the focus-lock button. You can then reframe the scene with the subject off-center (but at the same distance as when the focus was locked in) and obtain an in-focus picture.

In addition, autofocus SLRs usually offer manual focus. If you don't want to use the focus-lock control, you can simply switch to manual focus and adjust the lens by hand until the subject is in sharp focus.

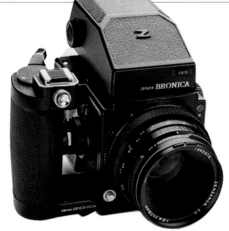

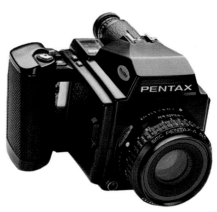

Roll films in 120 and other sizes consist of a strip of film backed by a longer strip of protective paper, both wound on a flanged spool. The leading end of the film is taped to the paper backing so both will feed through the camera together.

The major advantage of using a roll film camera is the large negative or transparency it produces. If you wish to make extremely large prints on a regular basis, you may feel the larger film format is desirable.

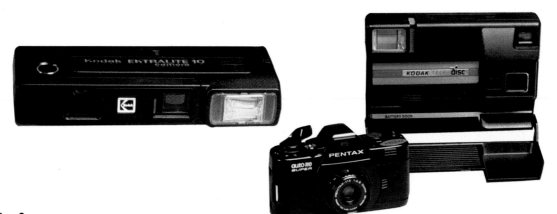

Roll-Film Cameras

Roll-film cameras most commonly use 120-size film rolls, which, depending on the camera design, can provide negatives sized from $1^5/_8$ x $2^1/_4$ inches (4.5 x 6 cm) to $2^1/_4$ x $3^3/_4$ inches (6 x 9 cm). Although there are other sizes of roll film, the 120 size is currently the most popular for roll-film cameras in general use.

Automatic-exposure 120 cameras include both rangefinder and SLR types. They are significantly larger and heavier than cameras made for smaller formats, as are their interchangeable lenses and accessories. The major advantage of using a roll-film camera is the large negative or transparency it produces. If you wish to make extremely large prints on a regular basis, you may feel the larger film format is desirable. Aside from yielding a larger film frame, this type of camera does nothing that cannot be done more easily with a 35 mm camera.

110 and Disc Cameras

These are pure snapshot cameras. They are simple to use and convenient to carry. With these cameras, the film is in a plastic housing that drops into the camera for easy loading.

Usually they have a fixed-focus lens, automatic exposure, built-in flash, and a built-in, close-up slide lens or a telephoto slide lens. The KODAK Disc 6100 Camera, for instance, has a built-in, close-up lens, and the KODAK Tele Disc Camera has a built-in telephoto lens. Disc and 110 cameras offer not only ease of use but extreme portability as they can fit in a pocket.

Shown here are a simple 110 camera, a single-lens-reflex 110 camera, and a disc camera. Small size and simplicity are their main features.

CAMERA CARE

Keep Your Camera Clean
Clean cameras work better and last longer than dirty ones. Although a full-scale internal camera cleaning is a job for a skilled repair technician, there's quite a lot you can do simply and easily to keep your camera in top shape.

Cleaning Materials
These are indispensible. They provide the only safe way for cleaning the camera and lens. Lens brushes are styled like small paint brushes or as retractable models in lipstick-like cases. The former are handy for cleaning the camera body. The latter should be kept in the camera bag for emergency lens wiping. Any brush you use on a lens should be used for that purpose only. Do not touch the tip of the brush with your fingers. Oil from your skin will collect on it and eventually be deposited on the lens.

Clean the Lens
A clean lens makes sharper pictures than a dirty one. Before each day's shooting, check front and rear lens surfaces. Any particles on a lens surface should be blown away. Don't wipe a lens that has sand or dust on the surface because gritty particles can cause scratches. If a particle won't blow off, roll a sheet of KODAK Lens Cleaning Paper into a tube, tear it in half and use a torn end to nudge off the speck.

If you get a fingerprint on a lens surface, first blow the surface free of particles. Then wad a piece of lens cleaning paper and moisten it with KODAK Lens Cleaner. Use the moistened paper to wipe the lens surface gently. Repeat the treatment with a fresh piece of lens paper as needed to remove the fingerprint. Never apply lens cleaning fluid directly to the lens. Fluid might seep into the lens

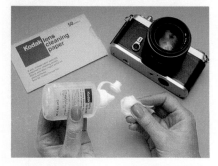

around the edges and cause internal problems. Never use chemically treated eyeglass tissue to clean a camera lens. Camera lenses have special coatings that can be destroyed by chemically treated tissue.

Clean the Exterior
Examine the camera exterior for dust and sand. If you spot any, blow it away with a squeeze-type air bulb. Always blow dirt away from crevices or openings in the camera body. The object is to move dirt off the camera, not into it. Follow with a gentle wipe-down using a clean, dry, soft, lintless cloth. When storing the camera, keep it in a case, equipment bag, or even a clean paper bag to protect it from dust.

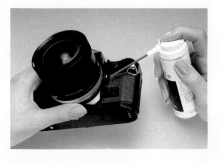

Beware of Heat and Cold
In hot areas, never leave a camera in direct sunlight for long. At the beach, cover your camera with a white towel or shade it under an umbrella. Never leave photo equipment or film in the glove compartment or trunk of a car in hot weather. Temperatures in these areas can reach oven-like levels. If your photo gear will be exposed to heat for long periods, keep it and your film in an insulated chest.

In a cold environment, keep your camera under your coat to keep it from becoming cold—the cold can sap your batteries of power. Remove it only long enough to take a picture. Do not take a cold camera indoors without protection. A cold camera in the warm indoors can result in condensation on the exterior and even inside the lens. Moisture and electronics do not mix. Before taking a cold camera indoors, place it into a plastic bag and squeeze out the air. After a half hour or so indoors, you can remove the camera from the bag. Should any condensation appear, wipe it off immediately.

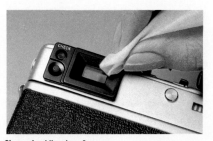

Clean the Viewing System
The better you can see through the camera, the easier it is to take pictures. With an optical viewfinder, check the eyepiece and front window or windows. They often become dirty and impair your view. Clean these surfaces as you would a lens. If the eyepiece lens has become oily from eyelash contact, apply lens cleaner on a cotton-tipped swab.

With SLR cameras, clean the eyepiece lens occasionally as just described. If you notice dirt specks on the ground glass, do not attempt to remove them unless the focusing screen is an interchangeable one that you can remove and reinstall easily. Remove the screen as outlined in the owner's manual, and try to blow the dirt specks away. If that fails, reinstall the screen, and have it cleaned professionally.

If you notice while changing lenses that the reflex mirror inside the camera body has become dusty, take it to a repair facility for professional cleaning. The mirror coating is delicate and should only be cleaned by skilled personnel.

Clean the Battery Contacts
Modern automatic cameras depend on battery power. If the battery contacts aren't clean, malfunctions can occur. Before you install new batteries in a camera or other photographic equipment, rub the battery contact surfaces vigorously against a rough-finish cloth or scrub them with a clean pencil eraser. Then scrub the contacts in the battery compartment with a pencil eraser to remove minor corrosion that may impede current flow.

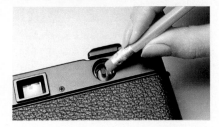

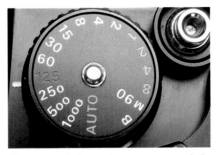

Shown as whole numbers on camera dials and displays, shutter speeds represent fractions of a second as you descend from 1/1000 down to 1/2. From 1 on they represent whole seconds. Each slower, marked shutter speeds lets in twice as much light. Each full jump (from 1/250 to 1/125, for example) up or down the shutter-speed range is called a one-stop exposure change.

THE SHUTTER

Next to yourself, the aperture and shutter are the two most important controls affecting picture outcome. Although they work in tandem to regulate the amount of light reaching the film to give correct exposure (see page 28), each also has a separate but equally important function that can greatly affect the appearance of a photograph. The shutter speed is a major determinant of whether moving subjects will be sharp or blurred in the picture.

The shutter is a curtain that uncovers the film to let light in to make a picture, and then covers the film to keep out light. The length of time the shutter stays open is normally quite short, from 1/1000 second to 1/30 second. Although a shutter speed of 1/30 second is slow by normal photographic standards, the shutter can remain open for several seconds or even several minutes when photographing in dim light.

The shutter speed largely determines whether moving subjects will appear sharp or blurred in a picture. Fast shutter speeds (1/1000 second) stop all but the fastest of moving subjects dead in their tracks. Even a galloping horse covers little distance in the 1/1000 of a second that the shutter lets light hit the film. If the shutter remains open longer (say 1/8 second),

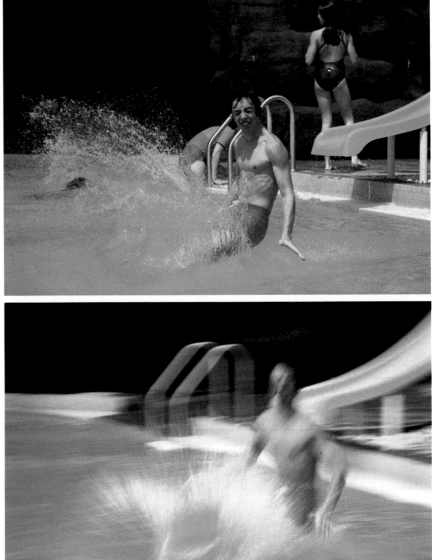

Neil Montanus

A fast shutter speed, such as 1/1000 second, freezes action. A slow shutter speed, such as 1/30 second blurs action. You must choose whether to freeze or *blur action. Sometimes blurred subjects make more interesting photos than those shown sharply.*

moving subjects form a blur that seems to flow across the photo. Both stop action and blur can be used effectively to portray motion.

When set on manual, the shutter speed is exactly as it reads on the dial or in the viewfinder. But when the shutter speed is set automatically by the camera, the speed is continuously variable and may actually be 1/280 or 1/650 second even though the nearest

speed indication is 1/250 or 1/500. This isn't important, just a little fact about how your camera operates.

The B shutter setting is for taking long exposures. When set at B, the shutter stays open as long as you hold down the shutter release. For long exposures, use a cable release (instead of your finger) to hold the shutter open. That way your finger won't shake the camera.

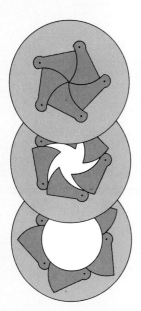

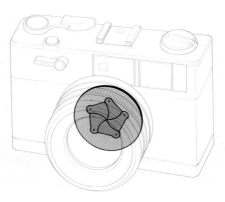

Regardless of shutter speed, a leaf shutter always fully opens to expose the film.

The Leaf Shutter

Most compact 35 mm cameras use some variation of a between-the-lens leaf shutter. This type of shutter is positioned in the lens barrel between lens elements. It is composed of several metal blades or leaves that swing outward to open. The moment the opening forms, the entire frame of film is exposed to incoming light.

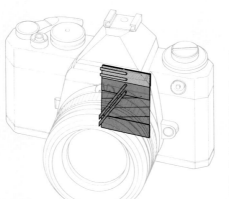

THE SLR SHUTTER CURTAIN

Virtually all current 35 mm SLR cameras use focal-plane shutters (so named because they're located just in front of the plane of focus—the film). Focal-plane shutters move either horizontally or vertically. They consist of two rolled-up curtains like miniature window shades or sometimes two sets of horizontally overlapping metal blades (shown at left). The practical operating sequence is similar in either case. At slow shutter speeds, say 1/60 second or longer, the first curtain or set of blades snaps open and uncovers the whole piece of film to light. When the proper time has elapsed, the second curtain or set of blades closes and covers the film again.

At higher shutter speeds, focal-plane shutters do not completely uncover the film frame in one instant. Instead, the shutter curtains form a slit. The slit sweeps across the film, "painting" a band of image-forming light as it moves. The faster the shutter speed, the narrower the slit.

Focal-plane shutter blades open fully for slow shutter speeds.

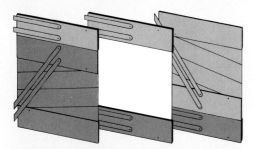

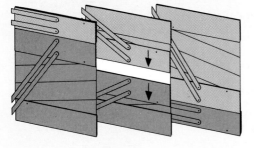

The shutter blades form a moving slit for fast shutter speeds.

THE APERTURE
(and Depth of Field)

The aperture is an adjustable opening made by a diaphragm inside the lens. It's adjustable so that you or the camera can regulate the amount of light passing through the lens for proper exposure (see p. 28) and so that you can control the sharpness of a scene from foreground to background.

The area of sharpness from foreground to background in a picture is called **depth of field**. The overall sharpness can greatly influence your perception of a photograph and the subjects within it. Too much depth of field can create visual chaos by burying the subject in an avalanche of irrelevant detail. Too little detail can leave important subjects poorly defined or even unrecognizable. The ideal amount of sharpness varies, depending on the subject.

The different aperture sizes are designated by numbers, referred to as f-numbers. The f-numbers are as follows: $f/1.4, f/2, f/4, f/5.6, f/8, f/11, f/16, f/22$. A small number ($f/2$) represents a large opening; a large number ($f/16$) stands for a small opening.*

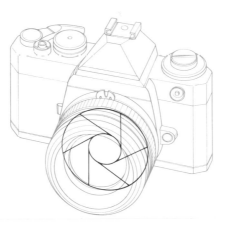

The lens diaphragm can be adjusted to regulate the amount of light passing through the lens. Specific settings are identified by f-numbers. Small f-numbers are associated with large lens apertures and large f-numbers are associated with small lens apertures.

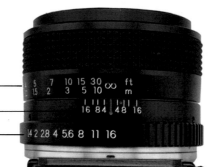

Distance scale ——
Depth-of-field scale ——
Aperture control ring ——

With many cameras, you can determine the size of the aperture by rotating the aperture control ring. The relationship between f-number and aperture size is shown at right. With most lenses, you can also set the aperture ring halfway between marked f-numbers to obtain an aperture of intermediate size.

*The f-number stands for the focal length of the lens divided by the diameter of the aperture. Thus if the focal length of a lens is 50 mm and it is set to an aperture 25 mm wide, the f-number is $f/2$ (50/25 = 2). If it's 3 mm wide, the f-number is $f/16$ (50/3 $\simeq$ 16).

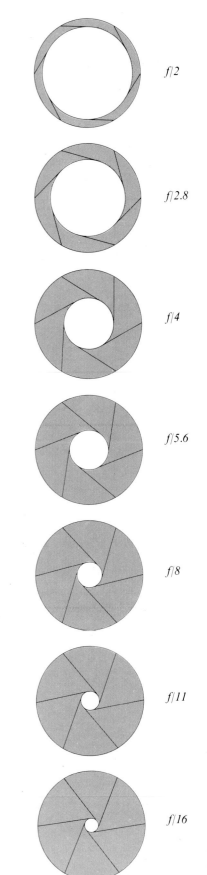

$f/2$

$f/2.8$

$f/4$

$f/5.6$

$f/8$

$f/11$

$f/16$

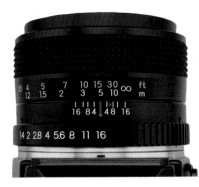

With this lens focused on 15 ft (5 m) and the aperture set to f/16, the depth-of-field scale indicates a zone of sharpness extending from about 9 ft (3 m) to infinity. The scale provides a quick check on depth of field at any aperture and focusing distance.

The size of the aperture is a major factor in determining depth of field. A large lens opening gives less depth of field or area of sharpness than a small lens opening. With a 50 mm lens focused on a subject 10 ft (3 m) away, an aperture of f/2 yields a depth of field of 1 ft (0.3 m); only the subject would appear sharp. However, an aperture of f/16 gives a depth of field of 9 ft (2.7 m), creating a large area in front and behind the subject that will also appear sharp.

With many automatic SLR cameras, the aperture is set by the camera or by you setting a ring on the lens, or a button on some cameras. With most compact autofocus cameras, you cannot adjust the aperture—only the camera can.

For different apertures, the actual depth of field in feet can be determined by using two scales on the lens barrel as illustrated below. Or it can be estimated by using the depth-of-field preview button. If you press this button while looking into the viewfinder, you can see the image provided by the aperture to be used for picture-taking. You can then examine the image to see which areas will be sharp and which won't—the drawback is that the image is small and may be dim, making accurate estimates of depth of field difficult.

Depth of field also decreases as image size for a given subject increases. Thus you can reduce depth of field by moving closer to the subject or by switching to a lens of longer focal length, which also increases image size. The reverse is also true: decreasing the image size on film by moving away or switching to a shorter focal length lens increases the depth of field at a given aperture.

USING THE DEPTH-OF-FIELD SCALE

The depth-of-field scale can guide you to the most efficient use of depth of field. For example, this scale can indicate how to show a flower bed sharp from front to back using the largest aperture possible. Here's how to do it.

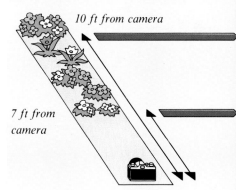

First focus on the farthest flowers. Note the indicated distance on the distance scale (green numbers at top). Here it is 10 ft (3 m).

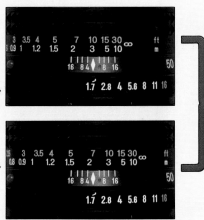

Focus on the nearest flowers and note their distance. Here it is 7 ft (2 m).

Adjust the focusing collar until you find the aperture marks for the largest aperture that completely encloses the near and far distances of 7 and 10 ft (2 and 3 m).

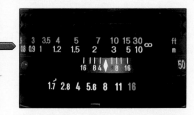

As shown here that aperture is f/8. Set the aperture ring to f/8. You have now focused the lens for overall sharpness of the flower bed. You have also chosen the largest aperture giving the required depth of field.

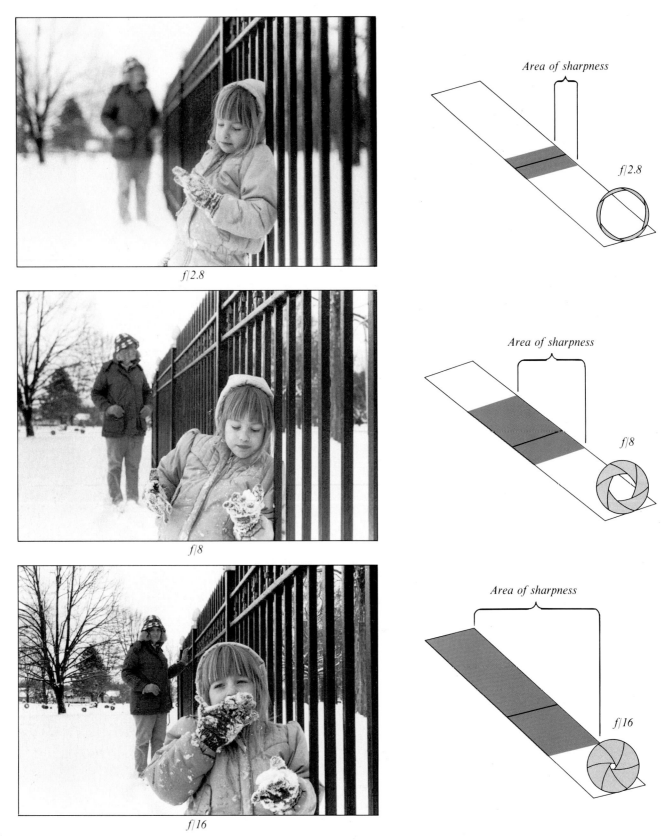

f/2.8

Area of sharpness

f/2.8

f/8

Area of sharpness

f/8

f/16

Area of sharpness

f/16

For this series of pictures, the lens was focused on the little girl, who was five feet from the camera. The aperture was then changed. When subject-to-camera distance remains constant, depth of field increases as the aperture becomes smaller.

PHOTO EXAMPLES OF APERTURE SELECTION

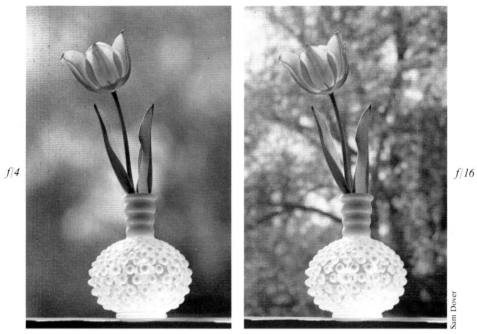

f/4   *f/16*

Sam Dover

*To blur the background so the flower
would stand out, a large aperture (f/4)
was used with a 135 mm lens. When a
small aperture (f/16) is used, notice how
the background distracts from the flower.*

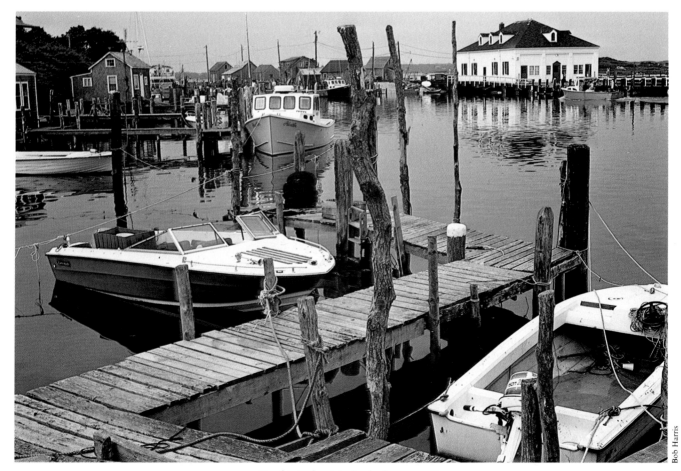

Bob Harris

*To obtain front-to-back sharpness, the
photographer used a 24 mm wide-angle
lens set at f/16.*

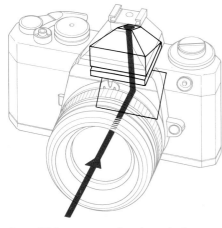

In an SLR camera with a through-the-lens meter, the photocell measures the intensity of light passing through the lens.

EXPOSURE: Getting the Right Amount of Light

Exposure is the amount of light reaching the film. Each film requires a set amount of light to produce a picture of the proper brightness. Depending on its sensitivity, one film may require more light than another. If a film receives too little light, the picture will appear too dark; it is **underexposed**. If the film receives too much light, the picture will appear too light; it is **overexposed**.

The amount of light reaching the film is controlled by the aperture size and shutter speed. Set to the sensitivity of the film (its ISO film-speed number), a light meter in the camera measures the amount of light in a scene. It then indicates the aperture and shutter speed that will deliver the amount of light required by the film. Either you or the camera must set the aperture and shutter speed. With most SLR and many rangefinder cameras, you can override the camera's automatic settings and vary the aperture and shutter speed. With most autofocus cameras, you cannot change the exposure.

Precise exposure is most important with slide films. With slide films, the film in the camera becomes the picture. With negative (print) films, a negative is made. The negative can be manipulated while making the print to compensate for minor exposure errors. In any case, accurate exposure is always recommended.

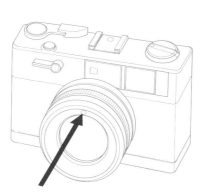

In a non-SLR camera, the photocell is often mounted on the front of the lens.

METER READING AREA

To accurately determine exposure for a subject, the meter should read light reflected from the main subject. A reading from an irrelevant area may cause over- or underexposure, especially if the subject is lighter or darker than other parts of the picture. The area the meter reads can vary considerably from one camera design to another. Meters are commonly classed as averaging, spot-reading, or center-weighted.

The owner's manual for your camera probably indicates the area your metering system reads. Keep the metering area in mind whenever you photograph a scene that is not fairly uniform in brightness. Make sure the part of the scene on which you wish to base exposure falls in the area of the meter's maximum sensitivity. If necessary, reframe the scene until the important subject area corresponds to the metering area. Then make a reading and hold it or lock it into the camera before reframing the scene for best composition. Only you know whether or not the meter is reading what it should be reading. The meter cannot tell.

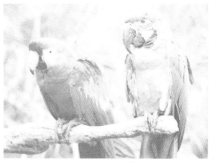

Overexposed

An overexposed picture has burned-out bright areas with too little visible detail and too-light darker areas with too much visible detail.

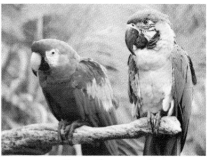

Correctly exposed

A properly exposed photograph presents a generally familiar rendition of the subject, with a natural-looking distribution of light and dark tones.

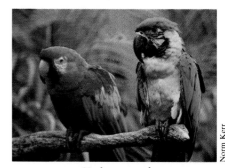

Underexposed

An underexposed picture reveals too much detail in very bright areas, and too little detail in darker areas, which tend to merge into black masses.

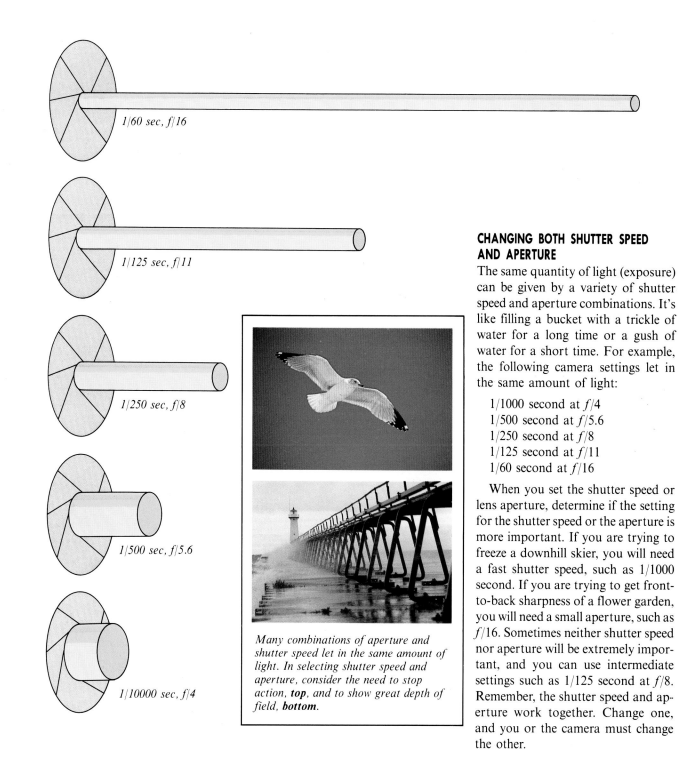

1/60 sec, f/16

1/125 sec, f/11

1/250 sec, f/8

1/500 sec, f/5.6

1/10000 sec, f/4

*Many combinations of aperture and shutter speed let in the same amount of light. In selecting shutter speed and aperture, consider the need to stop action, **top**, and to show great depth of field, **bottom**.*

CHANGING BOTH SHUTTER SPEED AND APERTURE

The same quantity of light (exposure) can be given by a variety of shutter speed and aperture combinations. It's like filling a bucket with a trickle of water for a long time or a gush of water for a short time. For example, the following camera settings let in the same amount of light:

1/1000 second at $f/4$
1/500 second at $f/5.6$
1/250 second at $f/8$
1/125 second at $f/11$
1/60 second at $f/16$

When you set the shutter speed or lens aperture, determine if the setting for the shutter speed or the aperture is more important. If you are trying to freeze a downhill skier, you will need a fast shutter speed, such as 1/1000 second. If you are trying to get front-to-back sharpness of a flower garden, you will need a small aperture, such as $f/16$. Sometimes neither shutter speed nor aperture will be extremely important, and you can use intermediate settings such as 1/125 second at $f/8$. Remember, the shutter speed and aperture work together. Change one, and you or the camera must change the other.

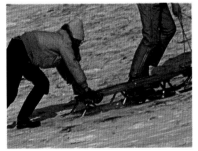

For white subjects or other highly reflective subjects, increase exposure 1 to 2 stops (slower shutter speed or lower f-number). If you don't, the subject may be greatly underexposed as shown above.

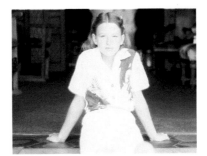

For scenes with a mixture of bright and dark tones, take a close-up meter reading of the subject and use the settings indicated. Failure to do so could result in the poor exposure shown above.

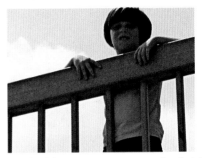

For backlit scenes or scenes with a bright background, increase exposure 1 to 2 stops. Otherwise the main subject may appear too dark as does this boy.

WHEN TO VARY EXPOSURE

Some people think automatic exposure means perfect exposure. That's not the case. Even advanced metering systems that don't simply sense light but compare it to a computer program based on hundreds of lighting possibilities sometimes need your guidance. In short, automatic exposure is designed to give good exposure for typical scenes, scenes of average brightness and reflectance, which, fortunately, most scenes have.

Your concern is with scenes of unusual brightness, darkness, or a mixture of the two. When confronted with such a scene, you should adjust the exposure by changing the aperture or shutter speed. Often you must shift exposure just the opposite of what you might expect. For example, facing the brilliance of a sunny ski slope, you might think less exposure is needed than indicated by the meter. Instead, more is required. The meter tries to render that brilliant scene as

average. Since average is considerably duller than the brilliant snow, it tries to make the snow gray.

One brief tip: When using negative film and confronted with tricky lighting, you'll nearly always be safe if you increase exposure 1 to 2 stops (use a slower shutter speed or wider aperture). The photofinisher can usually adjust for an overexposed negative when making prints. However, with slide film, you should bracket exposure as described below.

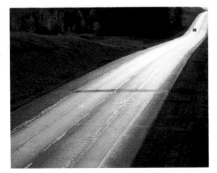

Normal   1/125, f/8

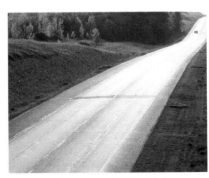

+1 stop   1/125, f/5.6

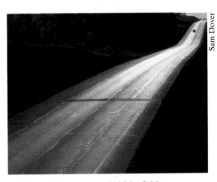

−1 stop   1/125, f/11

Sam Dover

Bracketing Exposure

Bracketing consists of making one exposure at meter-recommended settings, then making more exposures at settings over and under the first. It is best used with slide films, because they are less tolerant of exposure errors than negative films. Bracketing usually assures you of getting at least one good picture when faced with

tricky lighting. Full-stop exposure changes are normally used for bracketing. For example, if the meter indicates 1/125 at f/5.6, a full stop under and over bracket would include additional shots at 1/125, f/8 and 1/125, f/4. Or, if you like, you can use the same aperture and alter the shutter speed.

To bracket, take additional exposures at a full stop over (next slower shutter speed or lower numbered aperture) and a full stop under (next higher shutter speed or higher-numbered aperture) than the settings indicated by the camera's meter.

CONTROLS THAT ALTER EXPOSURE

Most automatic SLR cameras offer you at least one control for varying the exposure. If you use one of these devices, be sure to turn it off when finished.

If your camera has a film-speed dial, you can reset it to increase or decrease exposure. To decrease exposure 1 stop, reset the film-speed dial to a number twice the film's actual speed (from ISO 200 to 400). To increase exposure 1 stop, reset the dial to a number half the film's actual speed (from ISO 200 to 100). When done, return the film-speed dial to the correct setting for the film.

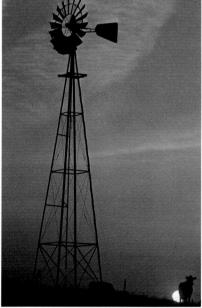

By underexposing to form a silhouette, the photographer created a dramatic photo. Altering exposure for creative effects works best with slide film which the photofinisher doesn't interpret. With negative film, the photofinisher may inadvertently undo your creative effects when making the print from the negative.

Robert Shelley, Jr.

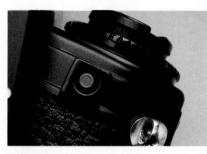

Backlight Button
The backlight button is typically on the front of the camera. Usually you must hold it in while taking a picture. It increases exposure about 1½ stops.

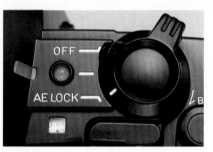

Exposure-Hold
Exposure-hold is a button or lever that locks in exposure settings at the moment the control is actuated. It is most often used for locking in settings based on a close-up exposure reading of the subject.

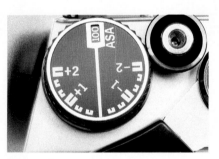

Exposure Compensation
This control is typically a dial atop the camera that you rotate to gain up to ±2 stops exposure variation. On some cameras, this control is a button. Either way, the automatic exposure system continues to operate but always biasing exposure to the setting locked in until the control is reset to zero.

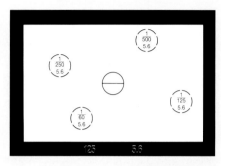

Special Metering
A few cameras offer an alternate metering method to gain more accurate exposure. One model compares scene lighting to a computer program based on hundreds of lighting situations, and adjusts the exposure settings accordingly.

Some cameras have a spot meter. Unlike the normal camera meter that measures light from a large portion of the scene, a spot meter reads light from no more of the scene than covered by the center circle in the viewfinder. Thus, you can selectively meter off the main subject without walking in for a close-up reading. One camera's spot meter lets you accumulate several readings from different areas of the scene, so it can then average them out. Review your camera manual if your camera has a special metering mode.

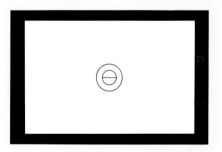

Manual Operating Mode
For cameras with a manual mode, you can simply set the shutter speed and aperture yourself. To increase exposure, use a slower shutter speed than indicated or a larger aperture (lower number).

TYPES OF AUTOMATIC EXPOSURE

Automatic cameras differ in the exposure automation (or modes) they offer. Some modes give only partial automation, requiring you to set either shutter speed or aperture. These are often referred to as aperture-priority or shutter-priority cameras. Others use a program that sets both shutter speed and aperture, and may offer several ways of doing it, emphasizing a fast shutter speed, a small aperture, or a compromise between the two. And a few cameras present you all these exposure options along with a manual mode in which you set both aperture and shutter speed. A camera that offers one program mode and an alternative automatic or manual mode will suffice for most picture-taking.

Whether cameras with many modes of exposure automation could be called decision-free is debatable. With them, you no longer simply press a button to take a picture. You first decide on the exposure mode. The more modes available, the more complicated your decision. If you just want convenience, choose the normal program mode. It uses moderate shutter speeds and moderate apertures. However if you enjoy exploring electronic variations, then you'll like a multi-mode camera—some offer up to fifteen alternatives.

When you decide the mode you want, set the mode switch. It is often located on or near the shutter-speed dial. With most cameras when you set the mode switch to a program, you must also set the aperture ring either to its minimum aperture or to a special **A** or **P** setting so that the camera can select the aperture as well as the shutter speed. Consult your camera manual for specifics. Explanations of the common automatic exposure modes follow.

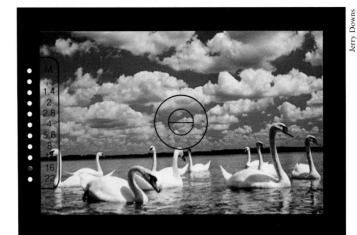
Aperture priority

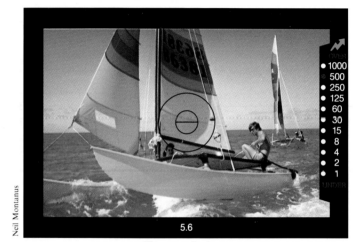
Shutter priority

Aperture Priority

You set the aperture; the camera sets the shutter speed. Choose this mode when depth of field is important. You may want a very small aperture (*f*/16) to give great depth of field or you may want a wide aperture (*f*/2.8) to give little depth of field so that the subject is sharp but the background is blurred. Or you just might want a moderate aperture (*f*/8) to assure that the subject will be sharp.

Monitor the shutter speed selected by the camera. Sometimes it cannot set a speed that will assure proper exposure, and sometimes it sets a speed too slow to stop action or to prevent blur from camera shake.

Shutter Priority

You set the shutter speed; the camera sets the aperture. Choose this mode when you need a fast shutter speed to stop action or a slow shutter speed for creative effects. Depending on the camera, you may have to set the aperture ring to its minimum aperture or to **A** so the camera can set the aperture. Monitor the camera indications to be sure an aperture is available for correct exposure. If not, choose a faster or slower shutter speed until the exposure falls into the range of available apertures. Also check that the aperture meets your needs for depth of field. You also may want to use a fast film to obtain faster shutter speeds.

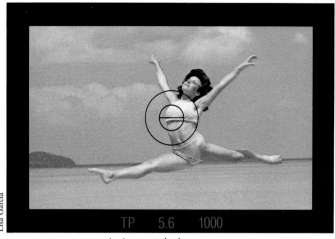

Action or telephoto program

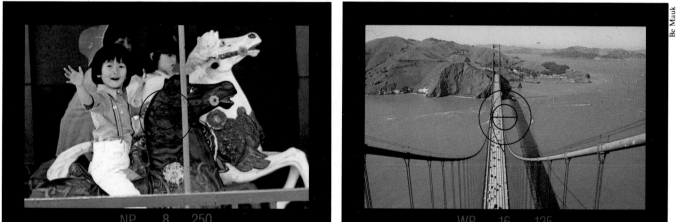

Normal program

Wide-angle or depth program

Normal Program

The camera sets both shutter speed and aperture, emphasizing neither. The program tries to choose a shutter speed that will stop moderate action and an aperture that will give reasonable depth of field. This is the ideal mode for snapshot photography. It works best when used with a medium- or even high-speed film, such as KODACOLOR VR 200 or VR 400 Film, that will give action-stopping shutter speeds and apertures with good depth of field even on dull days. This is the only mode on some basic automatic cameras.

Action or Telephoto Program

Designed to stop moving subjects, this program sets a fast shutter speed and an aperture suitable for correct exposure. The camera sets a relatively large or moderate aperture except under bright lighting, when a small aperture may be chosen. Typical exposure would be $1/500$, $f/5.6$. With some cameras, attaching a telephoto lens to the camera automatically puts the camera into this fast shutter-speed program. With other cameras, you must dial in the program.

Depth or Wide-Angle Program

Designed to give great depth of field, this program strives to set a small aperture. By setting a small aperture, the program tries to give you foreground-to-background sharpness. A typical exposure would be $1/125$, $f/11$. With some cameras, this program automatically turns on when a wide-angle lens is attached. With other cameras, you set the program.

33

Lenses

The number and variety of lenses available for 35 mm SLR cameras is astonishing. There are lenses with extra large apertures that gather the scant light inside an ancient abbey. There are lenses with extra small apertures that make a picket fence sharp from beginning to end. There are lenses with extra long focal lengths that bring close distant little leaguers being chased by fly balls. There are lenses with extra short focal lengths that embrace the near and the far. There are lenses that soften the wrinkles of grandmothers and make perpendicular the lines of skyscrapers. There are zoom lenses, wide-angle lenses, telephoto lenses, macro lenses, normal lenses, and more. But whatever the design, whatever the cost, all lenses share one common purpose: to form a desirable image of the subject on film.

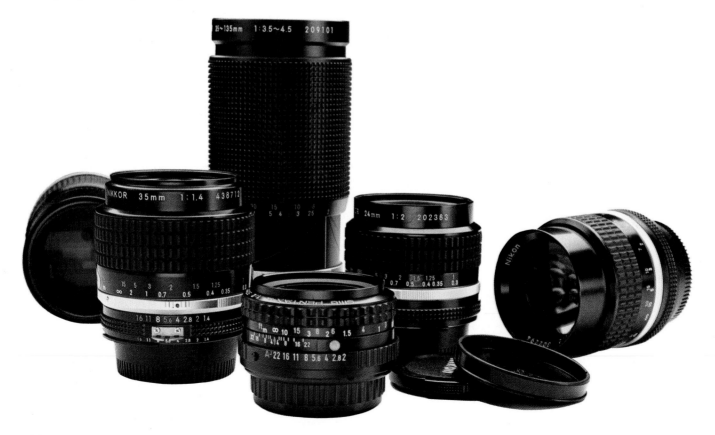

LENSES

The great advantage of SLR cameras is that they accept a wide variety of lenses. That's important because lenses are a creative factor. With a long telephoto lens you can render a setting sun enormous. With a wide-angle lens you can make it seem small and distant. Some lenses will suit your photographic style or interests better than others. Specialists in sports photography use telephoto lenses. Specialists in flower photography use macro lenses. As you become more familiar in photographing certain subjects, you'll learn if a specific lens will aid you or not.

Lens Focal Length

Lenses are classified by their focal lengths measured in millimetres. The focal length of a lens is the distance from its optical center to the film when the lens is focused at infinity, which for practical purposes is a distant object.

Normal lenses have a focal length approximately equal to the diagonal of the film format with which they are used. The diagonal of a 35 mm frame is about 43 mm. For 35 mm cameras, normal lenses generally have focal lengths anywhere from 40 to 58 mm. Common wide-angle lenses have focal lengths of 24, 28, and 35 mm. Common telephoto lenses have focal lengths of 105, 135, 200, and 300 mm.

For a given film format, a lens with a focal length significantly shorter than a lens of normal length is called a wide-angle lens. Any lens for a given format with a focal length longer than a normal lens is considered a telephoto lens.

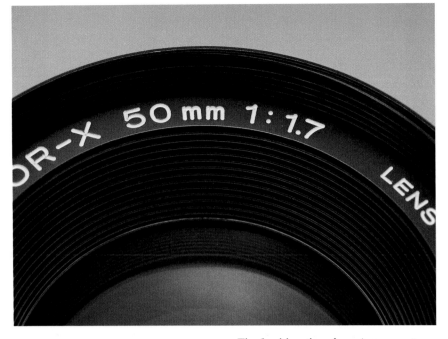

The focal length and maximum aperture of a lens are often marked on the front of the lens barrel.

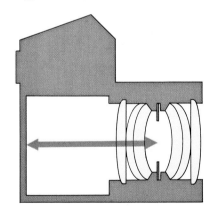

The focal length of a normal lens approximates the diagonal of the film format. The diagonal of a 35 mm frame is approximately 43 mm.

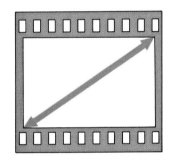

The focal length of a normal camera lens is the distance from the approximate center of the lens to the film plane when the lens is focused on infinity. With telephoto lenses, the focal length is often the distance from the film plane to a point in front of the lens.

Lens Aperture

The maximum aperture of a lens tells you about the lens' light-gathering ability. The larger the maximum aperture (the lower the numerical value of the f-number), the better suited the lens is for use in dim light. A lens set at $f/1.4$ admits eight times the light of a lens set at $f/4$ and can easily be used in dim light.

Although lenses with unusually large maximum apertures are ideal for existing-light photography, they are bigger and cost more than lenses with average-size maximum apertures. A normal lens with a maximum aperture of $f/1.8$ or $f/2$ will suffice for most photography.

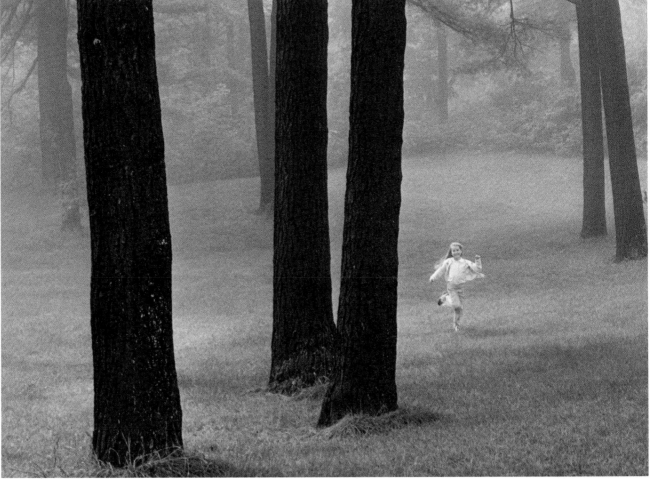

A normal lens most closely reveals scenes in a way that mimics human vision.

Terry D. Somenske

NORMAL LENSES

The most common type of lens, the one that usually comes with the camera, is called a normal lens. It produces an image with a field and perspective approximating normal vision. A typical normal lens has a focal length of 50 mm or 55 mm.

The popularity of normal lenses stems partly from the pleasant familiarity of the views they produce and partly from their ease of use. They take in a wide enough field to capture sweeping scenes at a distance, yet they can also isolate relatively small areas when you move in close. Most normal lenses also have a large maximum aperture, such as *f*/1.8, that makes them good for existing-light photography.

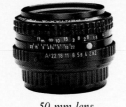

50 mm lens

Lens set for closeup   *Lens set for distance*

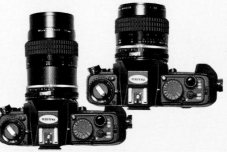

A macro lens can extend further than a normal lens, enabling it to make close-up photos.

MACRO LENSES

Specially designed for close-up work, macro lenses give extra sharp images of close-up subjects and can focus at close distances without special accessories. If you do much close-up work, you should consider buying a macro lens. These lenses can also be used for normal photography. Because depth-of-field is so shallow in close-up work, you should focus carefully and use a small *f*-stop, such as *f*/16. Use a tripod to prevent blur from camera shake.

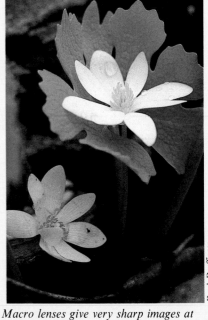

Derek Doelfinger

Macro lenses give very sharp images at close distances and focus close enough to let you make large images of small subjects without additional accessories.

WIDE-ANGLE LENSES

A wide-angle lens includes more of the scene than a normal lens. This makes wide-angle lenses useful for photographing panoramas and interiors.

The most popular wide-angle lenses for 35 mm cameras have focal lengths of 28 mm and 35 mm. Their fields of view are sufficiently wider than normal lenses to create a wide-angle look but are not so extreme as to be difficult to handle. Wide-angle lenses of shorter focal length, such as 18 mm, 21 mm, or 24 mm lenses, demand more care in camera handling. Minor discrepancies in leveling the camera create disproportionately out-of-kilter perspective effects.

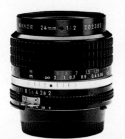

24 mm wide-angle lens

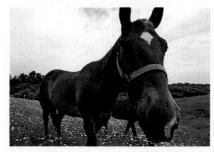

Perspective exaggeration occurs when a wide-angle or normal lens is used at too close a distance. In this case, an 18 mm wide-angle lens was used.

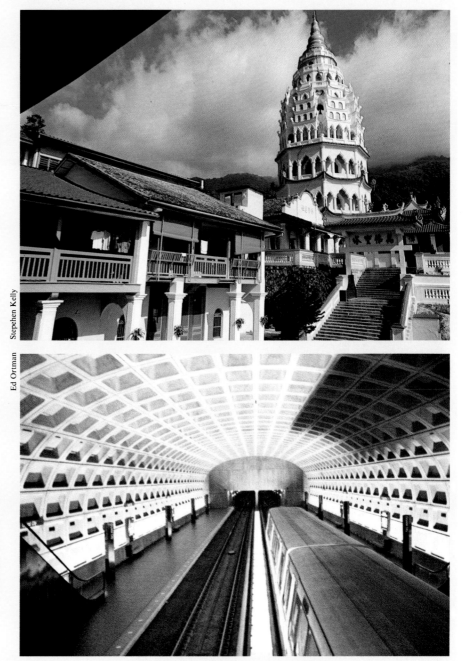

Stephen Kelly

Ed Ortman

Whether you are photographing a Buddhist temple in Panang, Malaysia, or the Washington D.C. subway, the great advantage of a wide-angle lens is that it can capture broad views.

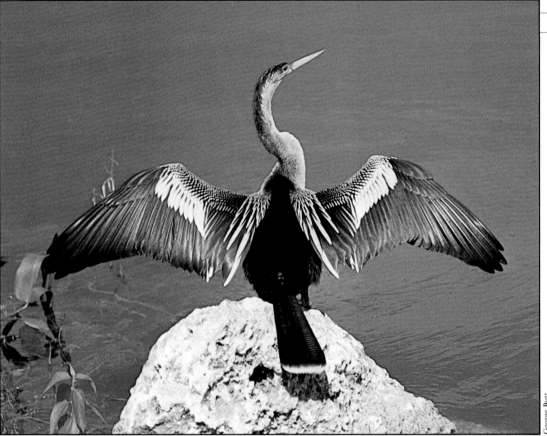

George Butt

TELEPHOTO LENSES

Telephoto lenses see a narrower field of view than normal lenses. They magnify distant subjects. Unlike a telescope, they don't magnify greatly. Their magnification is typically 2X to 4X that of the normal lens.

Because they magnify, telephoto lenses are most often used for subjects that are difficult to approach. Wildlife and sporting events are naturals for telephotos. Telephoto lenses from 85 to 135 mm are often used for portraiture. They agreeably flatten the face and when used at a large aperture (such as $f/4$) produce a blurred background that compliments the sitter.

The most widely used telephotos for 35 mm cameras have moderate focal lengths ranging from 85 to 200 mm. Image magnification is great enough to tighten composition attractively but not so great as to impose too many limitations. Lenses of 200 mm focal length and longer require faster shutter speeds because they magnify camera and subject motion along with the image. Compared with the moderate telephotos, they are large and heavy. For best results, use a tripod or hold the camera extra steady if you use a lens of 200 mm or longer at shutter speeds below 1/500 second.

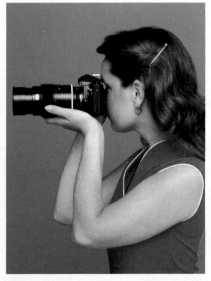

When using heavy lenses, place your left hand beneath the camera body like a shelf, with your fingers gripping the lens barrel. Often, you can focus with your fingertips without shifting your hand.

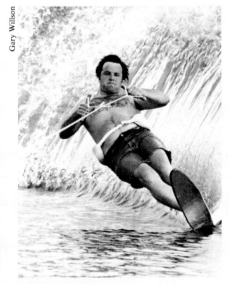

Gary Willson

Telephoto lenses are a must for photographing sports where you cannot closely approach the subjects. A 200 mm telephoto is often considered the shortest focal length suitable for sports photography. Lenses of 400 and 500 mm (and longer) are frequently used in professional sports photography.

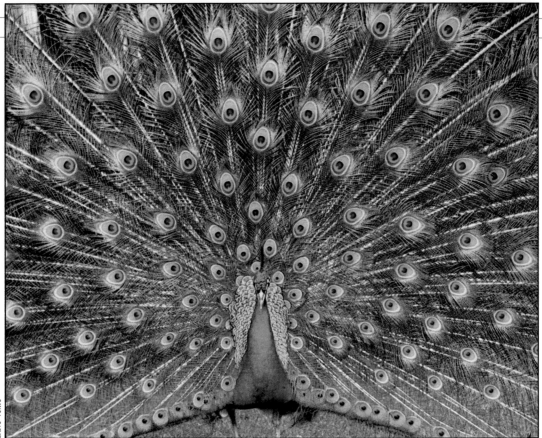

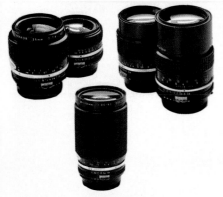

*A single zoom lens, **front**, can replace several single focal length lenses.*

ZOOM LENSES

Because of their versatility and convenience, zooms are probably the most popular of all lenses. With a zoom lens, you can stand in one place and by adjusting the lens alter the image size of the subject. In effect, without moving, you can come in close for a frame-filling portrait or back off to include the surroundings. Because a zoom lens has a continuously variable range of focal lengths, it can replace two or more conventional fixed-focal-length lenses. Zooms are available with focal-length ranges covering nearly every conceivable portion of the focal-length spectrum.

For 35 mm photography, one of the more popular zoom ranges is from approximately 80 to 200 mm, which provides about all the telephoto coverage a nonspecialized photographer

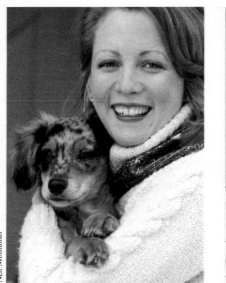

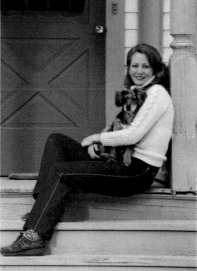

With a zoom lens you can stand in one place and change the image size by changing the focal length of the lens.

needs. Some zooms have a focal-length range from wide-angle to telephoto. A 35 to 200 mm zoom is an example. Other zooms have only a wide-angle or a telephoto range.

Aside from the convenience of carrying one lens in place of several, photographers like zoom lenses because they permit framing the image precisely without changing lenses or shooting distance. Many zoom telephotos also permit taking close-ups without any special attachments. When you zoom

from a short focal length to a longer one, be sure the shutter speed is appropriate to the longer focal length.

The disadvantages of zooms are that they weigh several ounces more than a fixed-focal-length lens (but considerably less than the several lenses they may replace) and usually cost more (but again, considerably less than the several lenses they might replace). Zooms used to be noticeably less sharp than fixed-focal-length lenses but now many are nearly as sharp.

Electronic flash

A century ago a photographer made a flash of light by igniting a combustible mixture containing magnesium powder. The results were clouds of smoke and frightened subjects. Today a photographer uses a portable flash unit that gives thousands of flashes and is powered by a few small batteries. The results are pictures made possible anytime, anyplace. Portable electronic flash units range in size from pocket models to handle-mount units that are about the size of a telephone receiver. Electronic flash units yield light similar to daylight. They produce light by storing battery-supplied electrical energy in capacitors and releasing it in a miniature lightning bolt generated in a flash tube. The resulting burst of light is intense and brief.

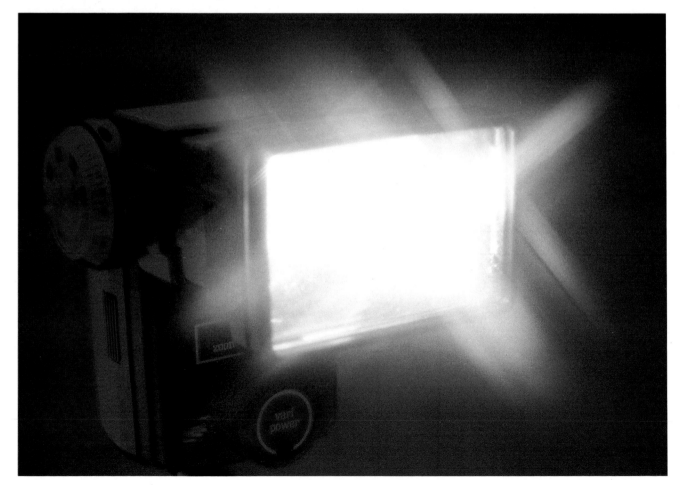

TYPES OF FLASH UNITS

Automatic and dedicated flash units are the popular types of flash used today. Although still available and relatively easy to use, manual flash units have dropped dramatically in popularity. Manual units emit flashes of light of the same intensity and duration every time. They require you to make all the flash and camera settings. Since you have an automatic camera, we'll concentrate our discussion on automatic and dedicated flashes.

Different models of flash units vary in power and light output. A unit's power is normally rated with a guide number for a certain film speed, usually ISO 100. The higher the number, the more powerful the unit. Guide numbers of 35, 90, and 130 roughly represent low-, medium-, and high-power compact units. With a low-power unit you may be able to take flash pictures of subjects only 20 ft (6 m) away. With a high-power unit, you could photograph subjects 80 ft (24 m) away.

Some flash units have a swivel head that enables you to point the flash in one direction, while keeping the light sensor aimed at the subject. This is most useful for bounce flash as discussed on page 46. Many units feature zoom heads that vary the dispersal of the light. The zoom head can funnel the light in a narrow beam over a longer distance for a telephoto lens or spread it widely over a shorter distance to evenly light the broad area covered by a wide-angle lens.

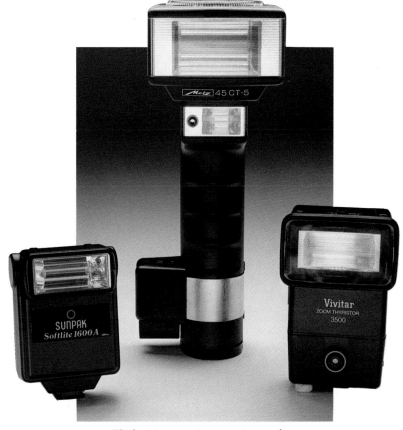

Flash units come in many sizes and shapes. Generally, the bigger the flash unit, the more powerful it is.

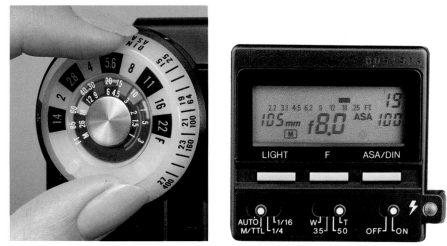

*Different flash units use different methods of providing you with information. Many units use dials, **left**, or scales, while others use a liquid crystal display, **right**.*

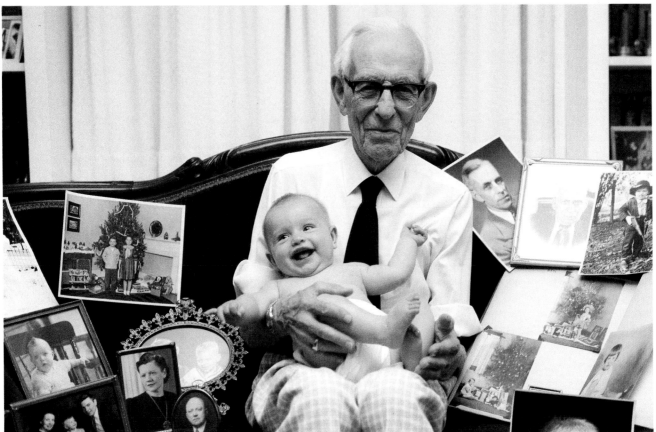

Derek Doeffinger

If the sensor of an automatic flash unit reads the light reflected from an unusually light area in the scene, average-toned subjects will be somewhat underexposed. Open the lens aperture at least 1 stop (for example, from f/8 to f/5.6) when photographing white subjects.

USING AN AUTOMATIC FLASH

An automatic flash is not quite so automatic as its name suggests. As the panel to the right explains, you need to perform several steps for successful flash photography with an automatic unit. Automatic units do have a big advantage over manual units. You don't have to change the aperture each time you move nearer to or farther from the subject. With manual units, a change in subject-to-flash distance requires a change in aperture. That's because a manual unit always puts out the same amount of light. Not so with automatic units. Because an automatic unit varies the light output automatically, you can choose from several apertures that all function over a distance range. As long as you stay within that range, you don't have to change the aperture. For example, with one model you can keep the aperture at f/8 as long as you are within 5 to 15 ft of the subject. Or you could keep the aperture at f/11 as long as you were within 5 to 10 ft of the subject. See your flash manual for specific distance ranges.

An automatic flash regulates the duration of its light output to give correct exposure. A high-speed, light-sensing system measures the flash illumination as it is being reflected from the center of the scene. When the subject has been sufficiently lit, the sensor turns off the flash. Depending on subject distance, the flash duration could vary anywhere from 1/800 to 1/30,000 second. Study your flash manual for details on how your unit works.

Many automatic units have a manual setting for when you wish to set the exposure yourself. You might do this for fill-in flash or when the subject is extra dark or light and could fool the flash sensor.

BASIC PROCEDURE FOR USING AUTOMATIC FLASH

1. Attach the flash to the bracket (hot shoe) atop the camera or to a flash outlet on the camera body by using a flash cord.

2. Set the flash shutter speed on the camera. It's usually marked in red (or designated by a lightning symbol) and typically is 1/60 or 1/125 second. Use 1/60 second if in doubt.

3. Set the film speed on the flash unit.

4. Turn on the flash.

5. Estimate the distance to the subject; set the flash mode that represents the appropriate aperture for the distance range. For distances under 20 ft several modes (thus apertures) may be available.

6. On the lens, set the aperture corresponding to the flash mode used.

7. Take the picture when the "ready" light glows.

USING A DEDICATED FLASH

Dedicated flash units can do all that automatic units do and more. They represent both the greatest sophistication and the greatest simplicity in SLR flash photography. Unlike automatic units, they are designed to work with specific camera brands and sometimes specific models.

When using a dedicated flash, set the camera in the auto or program mode. With the most advanced cameras, once you attach a dedicated flash, your only other task is to take the picture. With less advanced cameras, you may be required to make some settings. Once attached, all dedicated units automatically set the flash shutter speed. Many also set the aperture.

A dedicated flash and its camera form an integrated unit. Using special circuitry, the flash and camera exchange information. In addition to setting shutter speed and possibly aperture, a display in the viewfinder may indicate when the flash is ready and, after it has fired, whether the subject was properly exposed. Many dedicated flash units can also be set to automatic or manual for additional control over the aperture (thus depth of field).

Cameras that measure light from the flash passing through the lens give the greatest versatility with dedicated flash. With these cameras and a dedicated flash, you can make excellent close-ups, easily use multiple flash, and be sure of getting correct exposure with wide-angle and telephoto lenses. Most of these advanced functions are beyond the capability of a flash with a sensor mounted on its front. Because models of dedicated flash vary so greatly, study your flash manual to learn more about your dedicated flash.

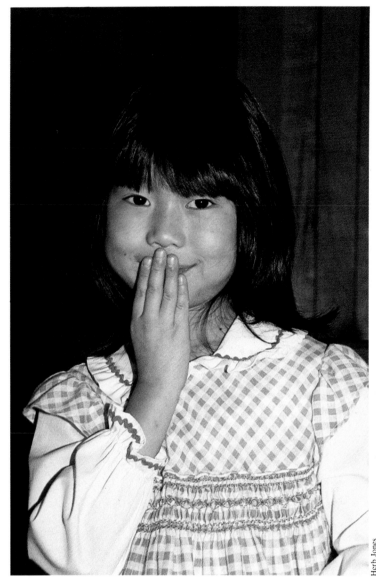

Herb Jones

Dedicated flash units make flash photography truly automatic because once they're attached the photographer is freed to photograph with little or no fussing and fidgeting with dials and settings.

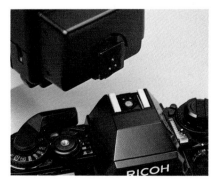

Multiple contacts in the flash foot and camera shoe indicate provisions for dedicated operation. Dedicated flash units are made to work with specific camera brands.

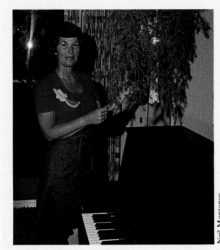

Do not aim the flash a mirrors or other highly reflective materials. The reflection of the flash will spoil the picture. By simply stepping to one side you can change the angle and eliminate the reflection.

QUICK TIPS FOR FLASH PHOTOGRAPHY

Check synchronization
Select an appropriate shutter speed, typically 1/60 second or 1/125 second. Use 1/60 second if in doubt.

Clean the battery contacts
Dry-scrub battery contacts with a clean pencil eraser to assure proper current flow.

Use fresh batteries
Replace or recharge flash batteries when the unit begins to take too long to recover between shots. Put a piece of masking tape on the flash unit and note on it the date you replaced or recharged the batteries.

Don't kink flash cords
If you use synch cords, don't kink or bend them sharply because the fine wires inside break fairly easily. If your flash fires intermittently, suspect the synch cord first. Keep a spare cord on hand.

Don't jump the ready light
When you're shooting action or working with an autowinder, keep an eye on the flash-ready indicator on the flash unit or the camera. Don't shoot before it glows or you risk noticeable underexposure. When the recycling time between flashes grows too long, replace or recharge the flash batteries.

FLASH SYNCHRONIZATION
To make a picture with flash requires perfect timing between shutter and flash. The flash must first fire only when the film has been fully uncovered by the shutter. This perfect timing is called synchronization. Synchronization is achieved by an electrical connection between the flash and shutter. Just as the shutter fully opens, it trips a switch that fires the flash. With 35 mm SLR cameras, the shutter must be set at a critical speed (or slower), typically 1/60 second, to uncover the film fully for successful synchronization (see p. 23). With many non-SLR cameras the shutter speed isn't critical (refer to your camera manual to be sure).

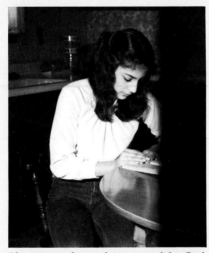

If set at too fast a shutter speed for flash synch, a focal-plane shutter cuts off part of the picture.

The focal-plane shutter used by SLR cameras fully uncovers the film only at shutter speeds of 1/60 (1/125 and 1/250 on a few cameras) second or slower. At faster shutter speeds, the shutter forms a slit that sweeps the image across the film. The moving slit would pose no problem if the flash produced light the whole time the slit was moving across the film. However, light from a flash typically lasts less than 1/1000 second. In short, the light from the flash has disappeared almost before the slit begins to move. Only the film directly behind the slit would be exposed. That's why the shutter must fully uncover the film to create a picture that is not cut off.

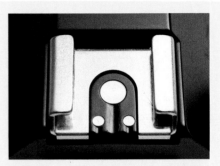

A hot shoe is a flash-mounting platform with built-in contacts that permit synchronizing the flash without a connecting cord. Only flash units with appropriately wired mounting feet can be used in this manner.

Hot-shoe synchronization
The simplest synchronization link between flash and camera is the hot shoe. A hot shoe is a camera flash mounting shoe on top of the camera. It has built-in synchronization contacts. When the mount foot of a flash unit designed for wireless synch is inserted into the shoe, a matching set of built-in synchronization contacts mates with the contacts in the shoe. No external wiring is required.

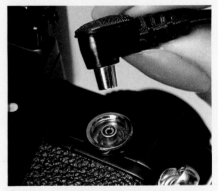

Many cameras have flash synch outlets that accept the plug of a standard synch cord.

Cord synchronization
Many 35 mm cameras are equipped with standard synch receptacles that accept plug-in synchronization cords. Such receptacles may be provided in addition to or in place of a hot shoe. The flash can still be mounted atop the camera. However, with a long synch cord the flash can be held or mounted away from the camera. Hot-shoe synchronization is easier. Cord synch is more flexible in terms of positioning the flash unit and varying lighting effects.

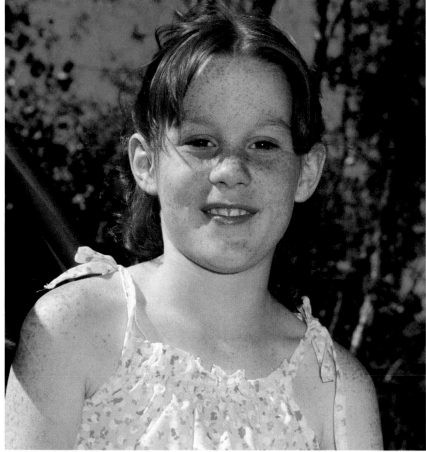

Neil Montanus

FILL-IN FLASH

You can use electronic flash to lighten dark shadows in brightly lighted outdoor settings. Known as fill-in flash, this technique is especially effective in portraits where shadows can mar a face. The technique requires you to establish an overall exposure that works for the daylighted portion of the subject while allowing the film to record enough flash exposure to open up the shadow areas. The procedure is most easily controlled with the camera and flash unit set for manual operation. If using a dedicated flash, refer to the flash manual for the proper procedure.

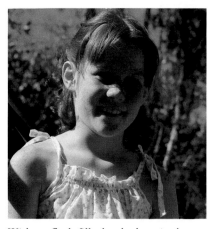

*Without flash fill, the shadows in the bottom picture obscure the girl's face. With flash fill, **top,** the shadows are lightened, clearly showing the girl's face yet retaining the feeling of the natural light.*

Fill-In Flash Calculation

For fill-in flash on sunny days, use a slow- or medium-speed film. KODACHROME 25, KODACHROME 64, and KODACOLOR VR-G 100 Films are good choices.

1. Set the flash to manual and mount it on the camera.

2. Set the flash shutter speed on the camera (typically 1/60 second). Do not use a shutter speed faster than the flash-synch shutter speed.

3. Use the camera meter to find the aperture required to give correct exposure. Set this aperture on the camera. If using KODACOLOR VR-G 100 or VR 200 Film, don't worry if you overexpose the film slightly.

4. On the flash dial, find the aperture that is one stop wider (next lower number) than that used in step 2. On the flash dial, find the distance corresponding to this aperture. Position yourself this distance from the subject.

5. Take the picture.

Here's an example using fill-in flash. With the shutter speed set at 1/60 sec, the camera meter indicates an aperture of $f/16$ is required for correct exposure. The photographer sets the aperture $f/16$ on his camera lens. To find how far to stand from the subject for proper fill-in flash, as required by step 4, the photographer refers to $f/11$ (one stop lower than $f/16$) on the flash dial and finds that the distance corresponding to $f/11$ is 10 ft (3 m). The photographer positions himself (or the flash) 10 ft from the subject and takes the picture. If you'd like facial shadows lighter, move a few feet closer than the recommended distance. If you want facial shadows darker, step back a few feet.

For maximum flexibility in adjusting flash versus background exposures outdoors, use a zoom lens and an extension synch cord. The zoom lens will let you change your image size easily. A long extension synch cord plus a light stand or cooperative person to hold the flash will let you vary the flash-to-subject distance.

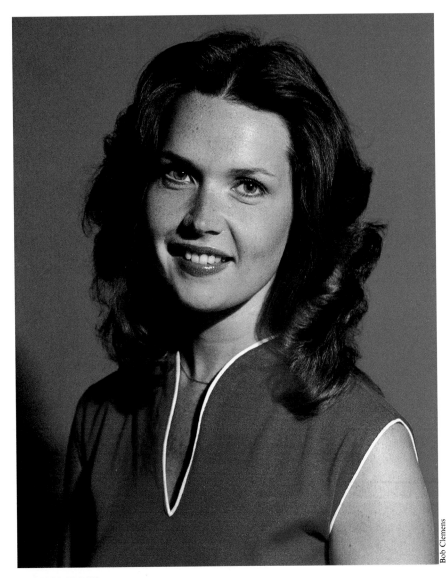

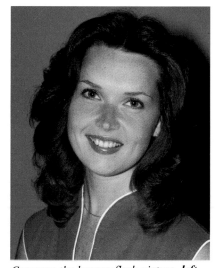

*Compare the bounce flash picture, **left**, to the head-on flash, **above**. You can see that bounce lighting gives a soft, uniform, diffuse light. It also gives a pleasing appearance over a greater depth than normal head-on flash.*

Bob Clemens

BOUNCE FLASH

Bounce flash consists of aiming the flash at a ceiling, wall, or reflecting card so that the light reflects onto the subject. Bounce flash creates much softer, more even area lighting than direct flash. Shadows soften and highlights broaden. Although ceilings and white walls work well, don't use colored surfaces if you are using color film. They will reflect colored light that will tint your subject. They can be used, however, as bounce surfaces with black-and-white film.

With an automatic or dedicated flash unit, you can use it in the automatic or dedicated mode only if the unit has a movable head or light sensor, or if the light sensor is mounted inside the camera. The sensor must be pointing at the subject while the flash

head points at the bounce surface. If you cannot aim the head and sensor in different directions, the sensor will turn off the light when the bounce surface, instead of the subject, has been adequately illuminated. If your flash unit doesn't have a movable head or sensor, use it on manual. If it doesn't have a manual setting, you can make it act like a manual flash by covering the sensor with your finger during exposure.

To use your flash unit on automatic, first determine the total distance from the flash to the bounce surface to the subject. On the flash calculator dial, find the maximum distance on the automatic-distance range for the aperture you are using. It should be at least 1.4 times the total distance you

just determined. If it is, proceed to use your flash as usual. If it isn't, you have several choices: use a larger aperture, move closer, use a higher speed film, or use the flash on manual. Using the flash on manual may be your simplest alternative. The procedure for manual bounce flash is on the next page.

Some automatic units have a confidence light that indicates if there is sufficient light for proper exposure. A confidence light is typically a green indicator that lights up if enough light reaches the subject when you test fire the flash. With bounce flash, a confidence light will be accurate only if the flash is on automatic and the sensor is pointing at the subject.

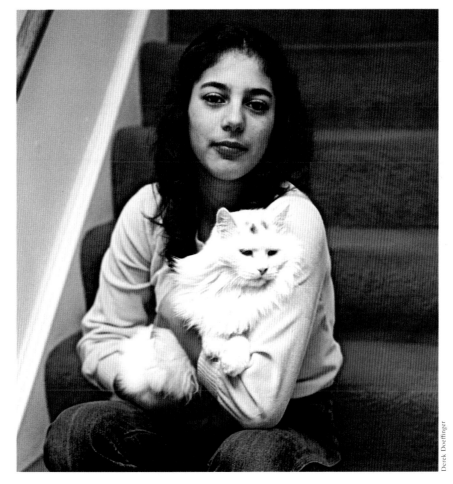

Derek Doeffinger

BOUNCE FLASH IN MANUAL MODE

To calculate exposure for bounce flash in manual mode, estimate the total distance from the flash to the bounce surface and from the bounce surface to the subject. Now find the aperture that corresponds to this distance on the calculator dial. Set an aperture that is 1 or 2 stops larger (smaller number) than the indicated *f*-stop. A larger aperture is required because the bounce surface does not reflect all the light striking it. Bounce flash is somewhat unpredictable, so bracket exposures. You might want to make a test roll, keeping accurate notes as you vary apertures to see how much adjustment is needed.

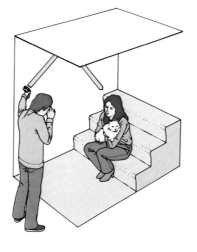

You can produce soft, even lighting over a large area by bouncing the beam of an electronic flash unit from a reflecting surface such as a ceiling or wall. The pool of light on the reflecting surface serves as a large light source. When calculating exposure for bounce flash in the manual mode, estimate the flash-to-bounce surface distance and bounce-surface-to-subject distance, and then add them. Set the lens aperture 1 or 2 stops larger than the aperture corresponding to this distance on the calculator dial (see text).

Accessories

Accessories for cameras range from the exotic to the indispensable, from right-angle lenses to sturdy tripods, from bubble levels to motor drives. As you specialize in certain areas, you'll probably find that your camera, although it is a precise and finely tooled machine, has limitations. You can push back these limitations— with accessories. Whatever you want to do with your camera, dunk it in the water or see around a corner, there's probably an accessory that'll help you do it.

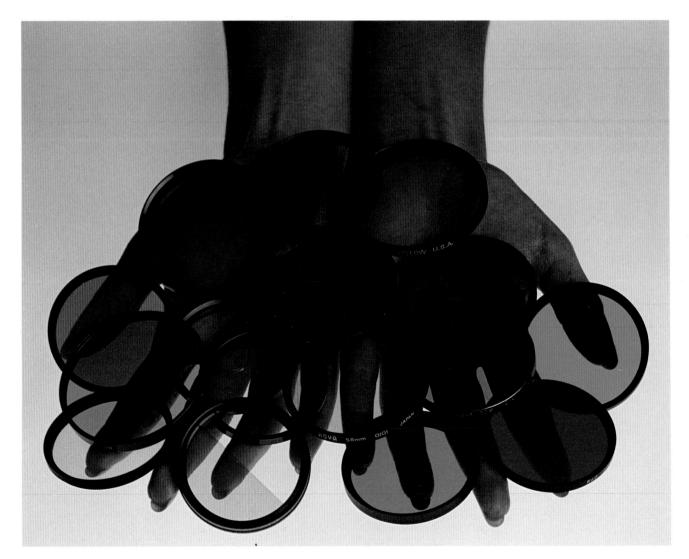

ADDING EQUIPMENT TO EXPAND YOUR HORIZONS

As your interest in photography grows, you will probably want to add to your equipment. Many photographers fall under the spell of the deep black finishes and smooth shiny surfaces of lenses, flashes and other gear. They become equipment buffs. You, too, may be tempted by the electronic flashes, zoom lenses, and filter systems beckoning with the promise of better pictures.

Should you give in? Only you can answer that. Although a piece of equipment cannot substitute for creativity, it can expand your creativity and inspire you to make photographs that were previously beyond your capability. To a nature photographer, a macro lens is indispensable. To a portrait photographer, a moderate telephoto is invaluable. Before you buy new equipment, analyze your needs.

A key question to ask is: *Is there a reasonable way to get results I want with equipment I already own?*

Another question to ask is: *How much will I use the new equipment?* A given type of lens or accessory may be available in models ranging from Spartan to deluxe. An economy model may be perfect for occasional use, but you might prefer to go first class with an item that will see frequent service.

Photography often poses problems to which there are multiple solutions. So it pays to familiarize yourself not only with accessories produced by the manufacturer of your camera but also with those available under other brand names. Independent manufacturers sometimes make types of lenses or accessories that aren't represented under a camera-brand label. And sometimes several different working procedures or degrees of convenience. Which is best for you may depend purely on personal taste or specific needs.

Tripod and Cable Release

If you make long exposures or shoot with long lenses, get a sturdy tripod. Tripods come in a profusion of designs and sizes and weights. As a rule, you will do well to pick the heaviest, most rigid tripod you can live with. Although the heavier units give greater stability, be practical in your selection. Choose one that won't unduly burden you when you carry it. A movable center post on which the camera can be raised and lowered without changing leg length is a great convenience, as is a camera platform that can tilt up and down and side to side as well as pan horizontally.

A cable release is simply an extension that allows you to trip the shutter without pressing the button directly. It reduces the likelihood of moving the camera at the moment of exposure. Some recent cameras use electrical extension tripping cables rather than conventional cable releases. The best cable releases are long and flexible. They lie slack enough and limp enough not to transmit minor motions of your hand and fingers to the camera.

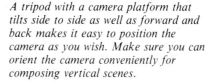

A tripod with a camera platform that tilts side to side as well as forward and back makes it easy to position the camera as you wish. Make sure you can orient the camera conveniently for composing vertical scenes.

LENS SHADES

A lens shade, or hood, attaches to the front of a lens. It prevents stray light from entering and creating light flares that degrade the image. Lens shades are made in different sizes and shapes to meet the requirements of lenses of different focal lengths. Shades for telephoto lenses are generally long and narrow while those for wide-angles are relatively short and widely flared. Only use a lens shade on a lens of the focal length for which it was designed. If you use a wide-angle lens shade with a telephoto, it won't provide optimum protection. If you use a telephoto lens shade on a wide-angle, it will cut off, or vignette, corners of the image. Lens shades also provide some physical protection for the front surface of the lens.

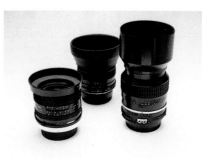

Lens shades come in different sizes and shapes to provide optimum efficiency with lenses of different focal lengths. Lens shades help prevent stray light from degrading image quality.

FILTERS

Polarizing Filter

A polarizing filter usually screws onto the front of the lens. It may be used to darken blue skies, to remove reflections selectively, and to increase color saturation. Polarizers are usually mounted in a ring that allows the filter to rotate freely. With an SLR camera, you rotate the polarizer while observing its effect on the image. As you rotate it, reflections in the scene may become subdued or disappear. When you see an effect you like, take the picture. Even when there are no noticeable reflections, minute specular reflections in a scene may cause colors to record weakly on film. Removing such reflections increases color saturation, or intensity, in the picture. Again, the effect is visible through the finder. Similarly, a polarizer is useful for intensifying the blue of a clear blue sky in areas at 90 degrees to the sun. If you don't have an SLR, you can still use a polarizer, but you will have to judge the effect by looking through the filter before placing it over the lens. When you see the effect you want, place it over the lens without rotating the filter further.

A polarizer typically absorbs enough light to require an exposure increase of approximately $1\frac{1}{2}$ to 2 stops, depending on circumstances and personal taste. Not all built-in meters can read accurately through a standard polarizer; some need a circular polarizer. Consult your manual or photo dealer for information about which polarizing filter should be used with your camera.

If your camera meter cannot accurately measure light passing through a polarizing filter, set the camera to manual. Make an ordinary exposure reading of the subject without the filter attached; then set the controls to provide $1\frac{1}{2}$ to 2 stops more exposure. Place the polarizier on the lens, rotate it to produce the desired effect, ignore the meter, and take the picture.

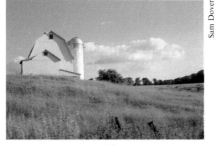

Sam Dover

Without Polarizing Filter

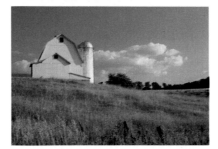

With Polarizing Filter: A polarizing filter is most often used to darken blue skies in pictures. While looking through the viewfinder, rotate the filter until you see the effect you want.

Skylight Filters

The No. 1A, or skylight, filter is used with color slide films to reduce excess bluishness that may occur in scenes in the shade or on overcast days. It also removes some of the excess blue associated with photography at long distances and with aerial shots. No exposure adjustment is required. A skylight filter is not necessary with color negative films because the photofinisher can adjust the color balance during printing. A skylight filter can also protect a camera lens from fingerprints, sand, ocean spray, and scratches.

The strongly colored filters used to alter contrast with black-and-white films can also be used to produced unusual effects with color films. This striking picture was made through a No. 25 red filter.

Patty Van-Dolson

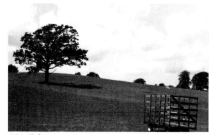

No Filter

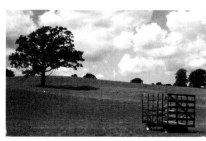

No. 8 Yellow Filter

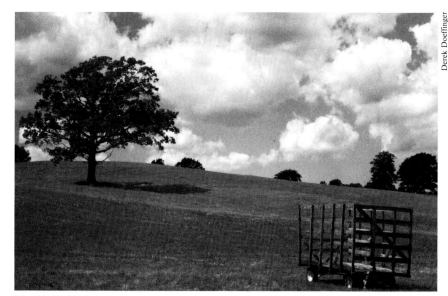

No. 25 Red Filter

Filters for Black-and-White Pictures

Colored filters in various strengths of red, yellow, green, and blue are used to selectively alter the contrast of black-and-white films. You can use them to lighten or darken objects of certain colors relative to the tonal values with which other subjects are recorded. They are most often used to darken a blue sky so the clouds appear brighter. The basic rule is that a filter allows objects of the same or similar colors as the filter to record lighter than normal, but darkens the rendition of objects of complementary color. The same filters can also be used with color films to create strongly colored special effects.

Most meters that read through filters will compensate adequately with the filters in this category, although exceptions can occur. You can check your meter by comparing the exposure settings before and after attaching a filter. The after settings should correspond to the exposure changes recommended in the filter table on this page. Consult the owner's manual for specific information about your equipment. And bracket exposures when seeking specific effects.

FILTERS FOR DAYLIGHT PHOTOGRAPHY
with general-purpose black-and-white films

Subject	Effect desired	Suggested filter	Color of filter	Increase exposure time by	Or open lens
Clouds against blue sky	Natural	No. 8	Yellow	×2	1 stop
	Darkened	No. 15	Deep yellow	×2.5	1⅓ stops
Blue sky as background for other subjects	Spectacular	No. 25	Red	×8	3 stops
	Almost black	No. 29	Deep red	×16	4 stops
Marine scenes when sky is blue	Natural	No. 8	Yellow	×2	1 stop
	Water dark	No. 15	Deep yellow	×2.5	1⅓ stops
Sunsets	Natural	none or No. 8	None or yellow	×2	1 stop
	Increased brilliance	No. 15	Deep yellow	×2.5	1⅓ stops
		No. 25	Red	×8	3 stops
Distant landscapes	Natural	No. 8	Yellow	×2	1 stop
	Haze reduction	No. 15	Deep yellow	×2.5	1⅓ stops
	Greater haze reduction	No. 25	Red	×8	3 stops
		No. 29	Deep red	×16	4 stops
Nearby foliage	Natural	No. 8	Yellow	×2	1 stop
		No. 11	Yellowish-green	×4	2 stops
	Light	No. 58	Green	×6	2⅔ stops
Flowers	Natural	No. 8	Yellow	×2	1 stop
		No. 11	Yellowish-green	×4	2 stops
Red, bronze, orange, and similar colors	Lighter to show detail	No. 25	Red	×8	3 stops
Dark blue, purple, and similar colors	Lighter to show detail	none or No. 47	None or blue	×6	2⅔ stops
Architectural stone, wood, fabrics, sand, snow, etc, when sunlit under blue sky	Natural	No. 8	Yellow	×2	1 stop
	Enhanced texture rendering	No. 15	Deep yellow	×2.5	1⅓ stops
		No. 25	Red	×8	3 stops

NOTE: If the exposure meter in your camera cannot accurately read light transmitted by a filter, first take an exposure reading without the filter attached. After attaching the filter, adjust the exposure according to this table.

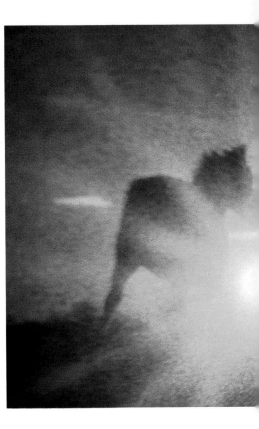

SUPPLEMENTARY CLOSE-UP DEVICES

Although a macro lens is the best choice for anyone whose main interest is close-up photographs, there are good, economical alternatives. Close-up lenses and extension tubes offer an inexpensive means of taking close-up pictures. Simple close-up lenses that fit over your camera lens like a filter are the photographic equivalent of reading glasses. Known as supplementary lenses, they allow the camera lens to focus closer than it can unaided. These lenses are available in different strengths, expressed in diopters, for different field sizes and shooting distances. They require no increase in exposure, but the camera lens should be closed down to a moderate-to-small aperture for sharpest results.

Supplementary close-up lenses can be used with almost any camera lens on which they can be mounted, but are most convenient to use on an SLR camera. With other types of cameras, auxiliary framing devices are usually needed.

Extension tubes are often supplied in sets consisting of three metal or plastic tubes of different lengths. An extension tube fits between an interchangeable lens and the camera body. Each longer tube lets you focus a little closer to the subject and make a larger image. All three tubes together provide the biggest image. With a normal lens, the biggest image with a full set of tubes attached is usually life-size. Additional exposure is required when using extension tubes. Through-the-lens meters automatically compensate the exposure. If you buy extension tubes, check to see that they allow you to use your camera in the automatic mode. Some do not.

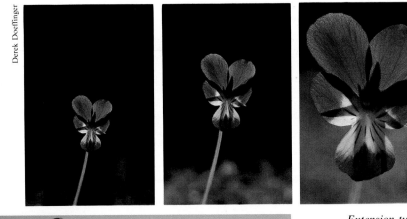

Derek Doeflinger

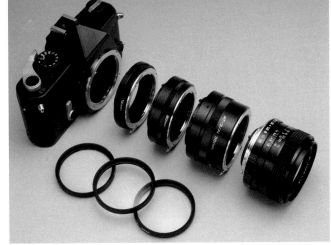

Extension tubes let you increase close-up image size in definite steps. All three tubes together usually provide a life-size image as in the upper right picture.

Shown at left are extension tubes in line with the lens and supplementary close-up lenses, which resemble filters.

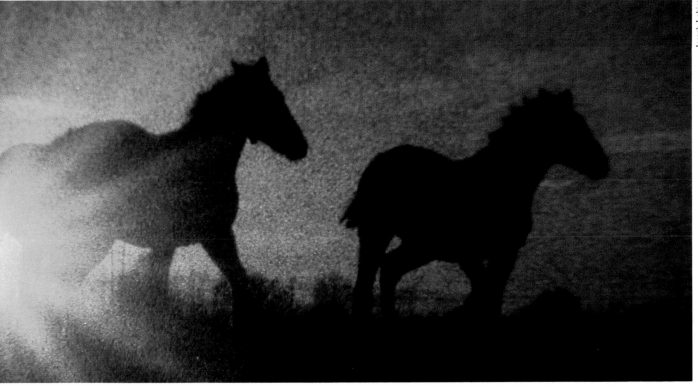

Joseph Lobius

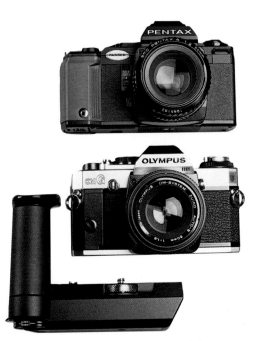

Many SLR cameras come with built-in autowinders to advance film and recock the shutter each time you take a picture. For cameras lacking built-in autowinders you can often buy a separate unit. They are especially useful for action photography.

AUTOWINDERS AND MOTOR DRIVES

If you are an enthusiast of rapid-action shooting, you may want to try an autowinder or motor drive, if one isn't built into your camera. Both are battery-powered, automatic film-advance mechanisms. Autowinders are smaller and lighter, and generally fire one frame per press on the release button. They may also have a continuous-run mode, in which the camera exposes and advances film at a rate of up to about two frames per second (fps) as long as the release button is held down. Motor drives are larger and heavier, and offer, in addition to single-frame operation, continuous-run speeds to five fps or faster.

CAMERA CASES AND EQUIPMENT BAGS

A camera case or equipment bag can provide welcome protection for your camera. If you travel light, with just a camera and few or no accessories, a conventional camera case provides cushioning against minor knocks and scrapes. Remove a detachable cover or take out the camera altogether while photographing to make sure the flap doesn't flop in the way of the lens.

If you travel with several rolls of film, a flash, and extra lenses, get a good equipment bag. A good bag should be sturdy enough to cushion the contents reasonably against minor shock and vibration and be large enough to accommodate everything with room to spare. It should be comfortable to carry and allow access to the contents without having to put it down. Look closely at seams and the attachment points for carrying straps and handles. The heavier your equipment, the stronger they should be.

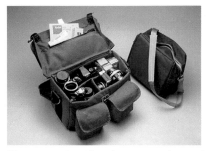

Choose a camera bag large enough to hold your commonly used equipment. Some camera bags have movable interior panels so you can design the interior to conform to the shape of your equipment.

About film

In the 1820s, Joseph Nicephore Niepce took the world's first photograph on a pewter plate covered with a solution of bitumen of Judea, a form of asphalt. The exposure lasted eight hours. In the 1830s, Louis Daguerre developed the daguerreotype—a polished metal plate with a silver-mercury image. A typical exposure lasted twenty minutes. From those beginnings has evolved modern film that can make a picture with an exposure of 1/1000 second. The variety of films is great. From high-speed and low-speed, from color and black-and-white, from negative and slide films, you must make a choice. Knowing some characteristics of film will help you choose.

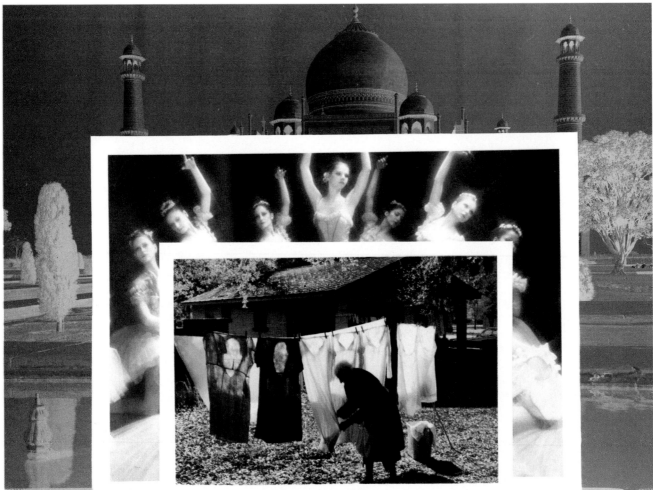

FILM SPEED

The speed of a film indicates its sensitivity to light. Speeds are expressed in terms of ISO numbers. These numbers appear on the film box and on the magazine, cartridge, or backing paper. The higher the ISO number, the more sensitive the film is to light. The ISO film speeds are classified into four groups: low speed (ISO 25 to 32), medium speed (ISO 64 to 200), high speed (ISO 400 to 640), and very high speed (ISO 800 and up). There is a predictable relationship between ISO numbers: A doubled number indicates doubled film sensitivity. A film rated at ISO 100 is twice as sensitive as one rated at ISO 50 and requires one-half the exposure in any given situation.

To relate film speed to the real world, follow this rule of thumb. On a bright sunny day, you can set your lens to $f/16$ and obtain proper exposure for a fully lighted outdoor scene by setting a shutter speed equivalent to 1 over the ISO film speed. For example, with an ISO 100 film and the lens at $f/16$, you would set the shutter to 1/125 second.

When you set your camera's meter system to the speed of the film, you are telling the meter how sensitive the film is. It will base exposure on that information. Be sure to set the meter to the proper ISO number.

If all your shooting will be in fairly bright light, you can easily use medium-speed films, such as

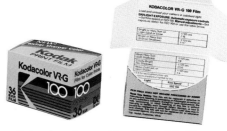

Printed on the outside of a Kodak film box are the type of film, the film speed, the number of exposures, and the expiration date. Printed on the inside of the box is exposure information.

KODACHROME 64 and KODACOLOR VR-G 100, or even a slow-speed film, such as KODACHROME 25 if you are not photographing rapid action. If you anticipate working in dim conditions or need maximum action-stopping capabilities, opt for a high-speed film, such as KODACOLOR VR 400.

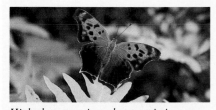

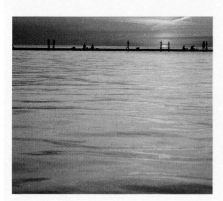

High sharpness is a characteristic associated with slow- and medium-speed films, such as KODACHROME 25, KODACHROME 64 and KODACOLOR VR-G 100.

SHARPNESS

Sharpness refers to a film's ability to record objects with great detail. Sharpness is best detected along the edges of recorded objects. Slow-speed films are generally sharper than high-speed films. The sharpness advantage of a slower film, however, may be negated under certain conditions by image

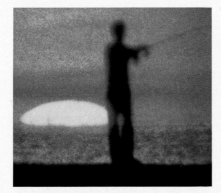

Graininess is the sandlike texture of a film that becomes visible at high magnifications. This example, taken on KODACHROME 64 Film, was enlarged approximately 50X. Generally, slower films display less graininess at a given magnification than faster films.

motion incurred by using too slow a shutter speed or insufficient depth of field resulting from too wide a lens opening. And the theoretical sharpness disadvantage of using a high-speed film may be outweighed by the benefits of shooting at fast shutter speeds that stop motion and at small apertures that yield greater depth of field.

GRAININESS

At high enlarging magnifications, exposed and processed film reveals a granular texture known as graininess. With modern Kodak general-purpose films, graininess may not be apparent at normal enlargement and projection sizes. However, graininess becomes detectable at extreme magnifications. Slow-speed films can be enlarged to a greater degree than high-speed films before graininess becomes apparent.

If you make enlargements greater than 11 x 14 inches (28 x 35.6 cm), consider sharpness and graininess when choosing a film. But always pick a film with an eye to stopping action and achieving necessary depth of field.

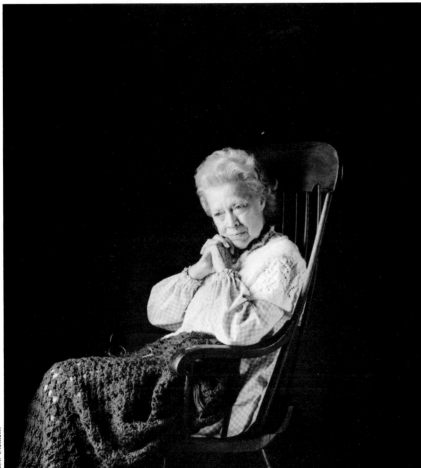

Bob Clemens

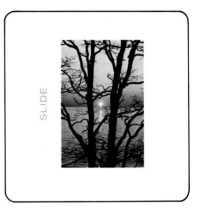

Color transparency films are used to make color slides. The same piece of film you expose in the camera becomes the tonally correct color positive you view or project.

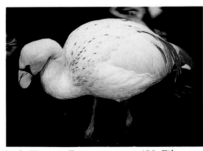

With KODAK EKTACHROME 400 Film, you can easily take pictures in the dark jungle of an aviary or at outdoor night events without using a tripod or flash.

BLACK-AND-WHITE FILMS

General-purpose black-and-white films are negative films that produce a tonally reversed negative from which a tonally correct print is made. Colors and tones in the subject are rendered in the print as shades of gray.

General-purpose, black-and-white films cover a wide range of speeds, from a slow, fine-grained material, such as KODAK PANATOMIC-X Film, ISO 32, to low-light specialties such as KODAK Recording Film 2475, ISO 1000. Both KODAK PLUS-X Pan, ISO 125, and TRI-X Pan, ISO 400, Films are good all-around films for everyday use. With its high speed, TRI-X Pan Film is expecially suited for action and existing-light photography.

Black-and-white films generally produce good results without filtration, whether exposed by daylight, electronic flash, or commonly used artificial sources.

General-purpose, black-and-white films yield a tonally reversed black-and-white negative that is used to make a tonally correct black-and-white print. Subject colors are rendered as appropriate shades of gray.

COLOR SLIDE FILMS

Color slide films are also called color positive, transparency, or reversal films. The film in the slide is the same piece of film exposed in the camera. After exposure and processing, it appears similar to the subject in tone and color and can be viewed directly, projected, or reproduced photomechanically for publication. Same-size or enlarged transparencies as well as color prints can be made from a color slide.

Daylight-balanced color slide films, such as KODACHROME 25, ISO 25, and EKTACHROME 400, ISO 400, are meant to be exposed by daylight or electronic flash. When exposed through appropriate conversion filters, they may be used with other light sources.

Tungsten-balanced color slide films, such as KODACHROME 40 5070 (Type A), ISO 40, and KODAK EKTACHROME 160 (Tungsten), ISO 160, are balanced for proper color rendition when exposed to various types of tungsten lighting. They may also be used with daylight or electronic flash when suitably filtered.

COLOR NEGATIVE FILMS

Color negative films, such as KODACOLOR VR-G 100, ISO 100, are intended primarily for making color prints. The negative represents the subject in reversed tones and colors. Only the final print shows the subject realistically.

Color negatives can also be used to produce color slides for projection or black-and-white prints. Most color negative films are balanced for exposure by daylight or electronic flash but may be used with other light sources. A few special-purpose color negative films are balanced for use with professional studio lamps.

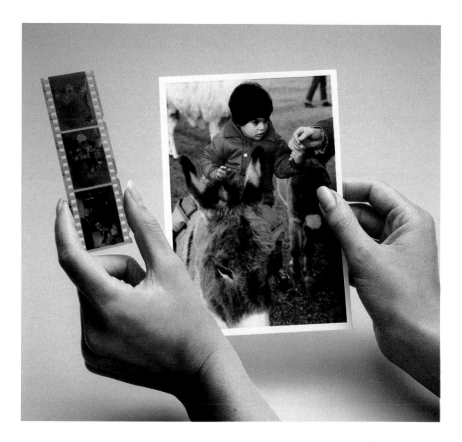

A color negative records the subject in reversed tones and colors. It is used to make a tonally correct print with realistic color rendition. If you are primarily interested in making color prints, use color negative films.

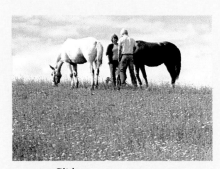

Slide, correct exposure

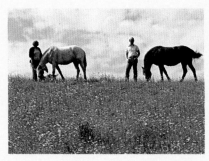

Slide, +1 stop

Slide, −1 stop

EXPOSURE LATITUDE

A film's latitude is its ability to produce a usable picture even if somewhat overexposed or underexposed. Different types of films vary considerably in their latitude. If you expect to make pictures under difficult lighting conditions, a film that exhibits wide exposure latitude is desirable. Negative films generally have more exposure latitude than slide films.

KODACOLOR VR 400 Film, for example, can produce good results with 1 stop underexposure and 2 or 3 stops overexposure. In large part, negative films have more latitude because print exposure can be adjusted during printing. But don't make a habit of counting on exposure latitude to make up for incorrect exposure.

For slide film the correct exposure, looks best, but pictures over- and underexposed 1 stop are also acceptable. Two stops of over- and underexposure, however, usually exceed slide film's latitude. Negative film can usually accept 2 or 3 stops overexposure and 1½ stops underexposure and still yield acceptable prints.

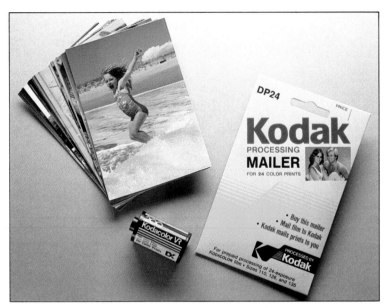

With Kodak mailers you can send your Kodak color film for Kodak processing.

PROCESSING SERVICES FROM KODAK

Eastman Kodak Company provides a variety of processing services for users of Kodak films. These services are available through photo dealers who can send in your film directly or provide you with convenient prepaid processing mailers. The services include processing Kodak color negative and slides and black-and-white films, making duplicate slides from color slides, making slides from color negatives, and making enlargements from slides and negatives.

A special processing service available from Kodak laboratories through dealers and via a KODAK Special Processing Envelope, ESP-1, effectively doubles the film speed of KODAK EKTACHROME 100, 200, and 400 Films. (You cannot double the speed of KODACHROME or KODACOLOR Films). For instance, you can double the speed of EKTACHROME 200 Film to ISO 400 or of EKTACHROME 400 Film to ISO 800. You would do this when you badly need a faster shutter speed or smaller aperture—typically in dim lighting. The whole roll must be shot at the faster speed, and you should tell your dealer that you doubled the film's speed. The dealer will then order the correct processing for the film. Increasing the speed results in contrastier colors and slightly grainier images. This service applies only to 35 mm and 120 roll films.

For best results, have film processed as soon as possible after exposure.

DX-Coding

To enable camera manufacturers to make automatic cameras even more automatic, Kodak placed a checkerboard code on the outside of its film magazines. A camera designed to read this code will automatically set the film speed, relieving you of a task that if overlooked could result in poorly exposed pictures. The code also gives the number of frames on the roll and the exposure latitude of the film.

By sensing the number of frames on a roll, the camera can keep count of exposures shot with an electronic display, indicate when to rewind, or rewind automatically when the last

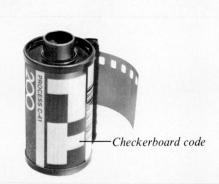

Checkerboard code

frame is exposed. A camera could also automatically adjust for exposure latitude of the film in the camera. Slide films have to be accurately exposed. Thus, under certain conditions the camera might discourage the photographer from taking a picture if slide film is in the camera. However, under the same conditions with negative film, the camera would read that it has greater exposure latitude and would likely produce acceptable prints.

A bar code on the magazine and coding on the tongue and edges of the film give information that aids the photofinisher in producing even better prints and slides from Kodak films.

Choosing a Film

Once you decide whether to use print or slide film, you have to decide what film speed is appropriate for the intended subject. If film speed is insufficient, you may not be able to capture the scene. So always choose a film fast enough to get the picture.

If you plan on photographing subjects outdoors by daylight, you'll probably want a medium-speed film, such as KODACOLOR VR-G 100. If you expect to be photographing inside museums, sports arenas, or other existing-light locations, you'll need a fast film, such as KODACOLOR VR 1000. When you expect to photograph both in dim and bright locations, or to photograph both fast-moving and unmoving subjects, compromise with your film choice. KODACOLOR VR 400 Film, for instance, works well indoors and out, and it gives quite sharp images. KODACOLOR VR 200 and VR 400 Films are good all-purpose films. They are fast enough to cover many situations and sharp enough to give you excellent results.

Although graininess increases as film speed does, films are now so fine-grained that graininess usually becomes a factor only if you regularly make big enlargements. But if you do expect to make big enlargements of a certain subject, take advantage of the fine-grain of lower speed films, such as KODACOLOR VR-G 100, which is Kodak's sharpest color negative film. If you want to learn more about films, read *KODAK Films—Color and Black-and-White*.

For extra sharpness and rich colors, the photographer used KODACOLOR VRG-100 Film to photograph the rose.

A 400-speed film is versatile enough to bridge exposures from daylight to existing light. Here it was used indoors without flash to photograph an aerobics class. It could just as easily be used outdoors for photographing action or scenics.

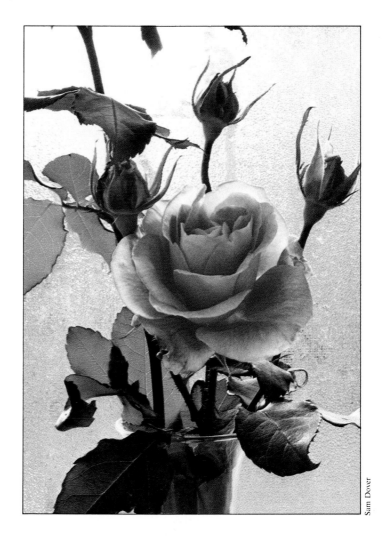

Sam Dover

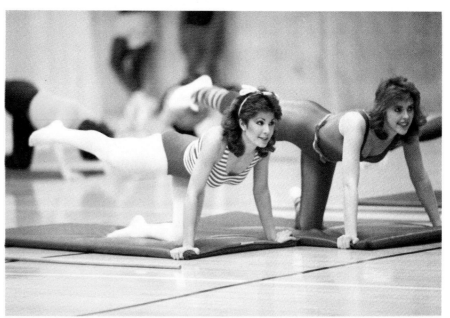

Elements of the picture

Understanding your equipment and film only starts you on the road to taking good pictures. To complete your journey you need an awareness and understanding of the photographic elements of a scene that can make a good picture. Chief among the photographic elements is the very one which makes possible both photography and sight: light

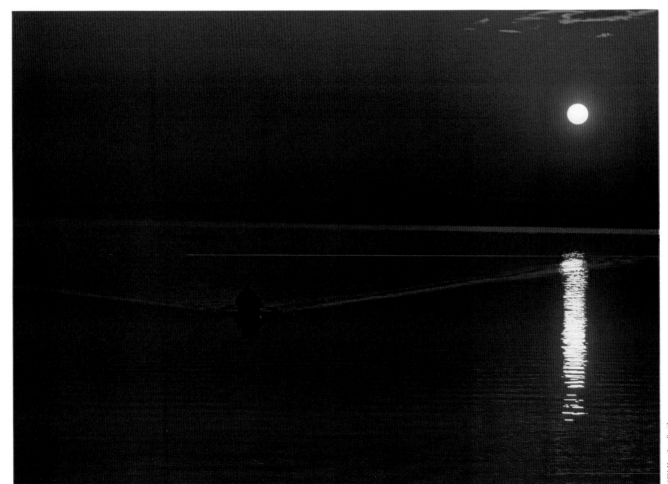

UNDERSTANDING THE ELEMENTS

The elements of the picture are not abstractions but are real things in the world as readily perceived as a rising full moon. When the presence of one of these elements stirs you like a moonrise you'll know that you have been properly sensitized. Until then, discipline yourself to analyze consciously how the elements in the scene before you can best be used.

What are these elements? The most obvious but least considered is light. Although there are as many varieties of light as there are paint chips in a paint store, we take light so for granted that we are often at a loss to describe it beyond saying it's bright or dim. In photography, light cannot be taken for granted. Other important elements are color and texture.

DIRECTION OF LIGHT

Light can come from the front, from the back, from the side, from above, even from below, and countless positions intermediate to all of these. Frontlighting, sidelighting, backlighting, and toplighting are the four most important directions of lighting. Each change in lighting position changes the appearance of the subject and its apparent relationship to other parts of the scene.

The shadows resulting from light are as important as the highlights. The highlights reveal detail. The shadows veil detail. Together, highlights and shadows define form and texture.

A subject that appears lacklustre and lifeless from one lighting direction may appear sparkling and spirited under light from another direction.

Frontlighting

Light that illuminates the subject from the position of the camera is called frontlighting. The sun shining from behind you during picture-taking gives frontlighting. Frontlighting illuminates the side of the subject facing the lens and casts shadows behind the subject, where they are largely unseen by the camera. Without shadows subjects look less three-dimensional than they are. The even, shadowless light of frontlighting results in flat-looking subjects.

Automatic exposure systems handle frontlighting quite well. Care is required, however, for highly reflective or nonreflective subjects, as well as normal subjects against lighter or darker backgrounds.

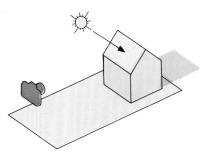

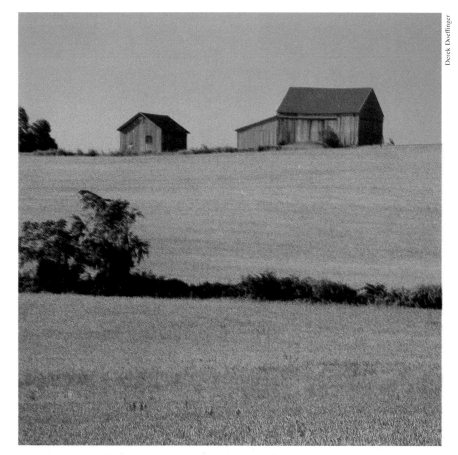

Derek Doeffinger

Frontlighted, a subject looks somewhat flat because few shadows are visible to camera. Subtle colors may be bleached out.

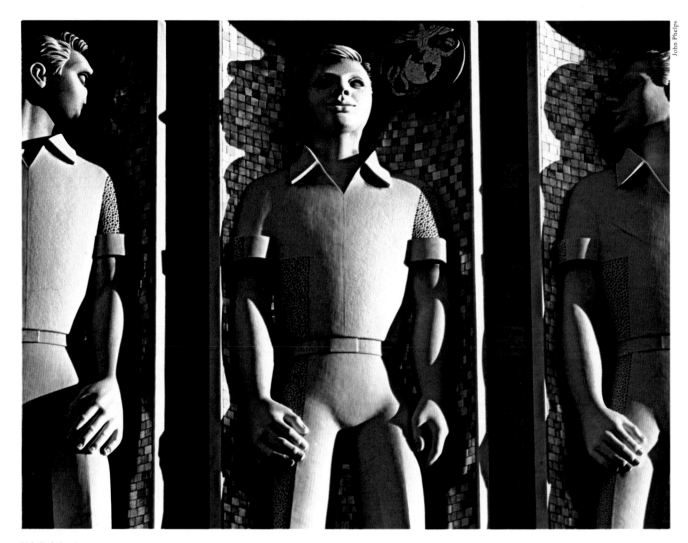

John Phelps

Sidelighting

Light that comes from either side of the subject and skims the surface is called sidelighting. Both the highlights and their corresponding shadows are visible from the camera position.

Sidelighting emphasizes form and texture. With it, the furrows of a plowed field stand out like miniature mountain ranges. A variation of sidelighting, with the light source high and located about halfway between direct sidelighting and direct frontlighting, is often used for photographing people. It models the facial features better than frontlighting, yet doesn't throw half the face in shadow, as does pure sidelighting.

When faced with sidelighting, automatic exposure systems usually, but not always, produce correctly exposed pictures. Sidelighted subjects seldom pose a problem if they show an even mixture of shadows and highlights. However, be alert when a massive highlight area adjoins a massive pool of shadow. In such cases, determine whether you want to increase detail in the shadow or maintain detail in the highlight. For more shadow detail open up $\frac{1}{2}$ or 1 stop from the meter reading. To preserve highlight detail, close down $\frac{1}{2}$ or 1 stop from the meter reading. Bracket when in doubt.

Sidelight skims across a subject emphasizing its surface characteristics. If a large shadow is present in the scene, decrease exposure to obtain normal rendition of the bright areas.

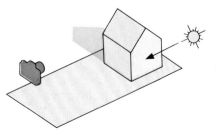

Backlighting

Backlighting occurs when the light source is behind the subject. Shadows stretch forward toward the camera, creating the illusion of great depth. A rim of light outlines subjects in the scene and separates them from each other and the shadows. The separation enhances the feeling that multiple planes exist within the photograph. The air and translucent subjects such as flowers and blades of grass seem to glow. With backlighting you can create bold, dramatic pictures. Underexpose to make silhouettes. Play the long shadows against the glowing highlights to make bold patterns.

Automatic exposure systems often need help with backlighting. While metering, be sure that the sun or any other light source is not shining directly into the lens. Otherwise underexposure results. Either frame the picture with the light source outside the view of the lens or hide the light source behind a tree or building. The meter should now give good exposure. These steps also reduce the like-

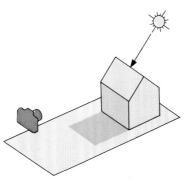

lihood of flare showing up in your pictures as bright streaks or hot spots.

When photographing backlighted scenes with slide film it is always good to bracket 1 or 2 stops either way from what the meter suggests. With negative film simply increase exposure by 1 or 2 stops. When taking backlighted portraits you'll want to show detail in the face. The easiest way to increase facial detail is to increase exposure by $1\frac{1}{2}$ stops. However, this method will overexpose the highlights. To provide facial detail yet preserve the highlights, add light to the face with reflectors or fill-in flash.

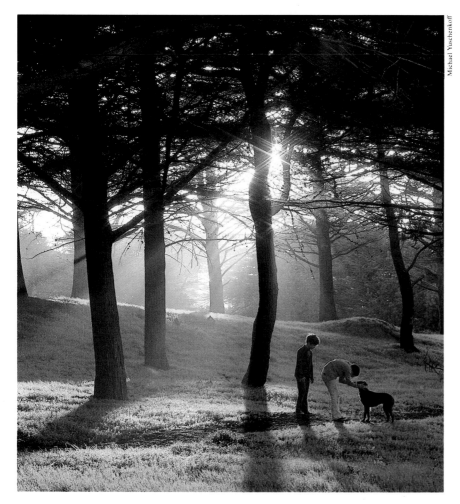

Michael Yuschenkoff

Backlighting creates the illusion of multiple planes in a photograph. Shadows cast toward the camera enhance the illusion of depth.

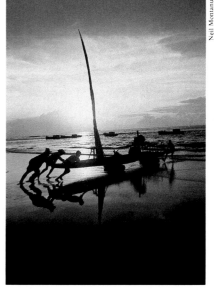

Neil Montanus

To produce a silhouette, set the exposure for the bright background behind the subject.

Toplighting

The overhead sun or a ceiling light fixture produces toplighting. Top-lighting fully illuminates only upper surfaces of objects. Toplighting poses no problems to automatic exposure systems because it generally illuminates large areas quite evenly. This evenness, however, may result in somewhat bland landscapes that lack a feeling of depth.

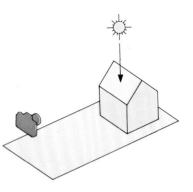

Toplighting creates bland effects because it reduces the feeling of depth in outdoor scenes.

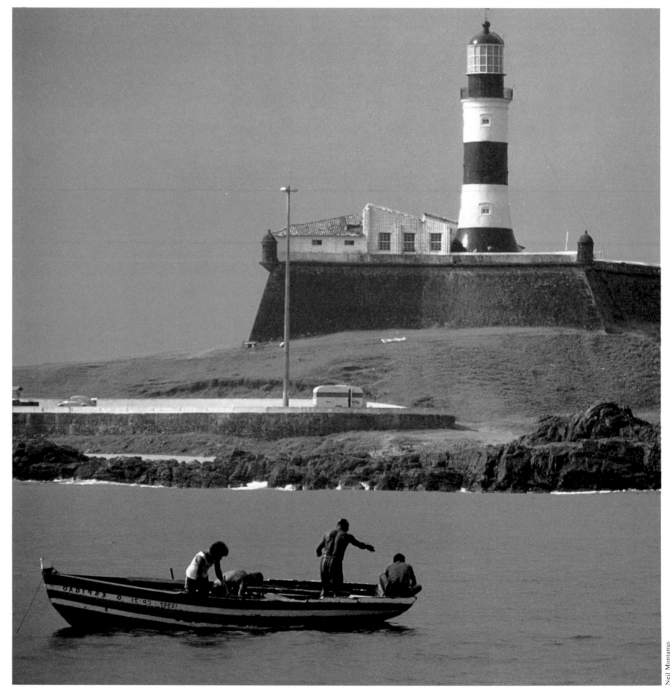

HARD LIGHT AND SOFT LIGHT

As important as the direction of light is the hardness or softness of light. A hard light is directional. It produces brilliant highlights and intense shadows. The bright sun in a cloudless sky gives hard light. Soft, or diffused, lights are less directional. They produce fewer glaring highlights and less intense shadows. Transitions from light to dark are gradual. An overcast sky gives soft light. Hard lighting produces sparkling, often contrasty pictures. Soft light yields pictures with a smoother, gentler look.

The quality of daylight can change quickly and drastically. If the light isn't what you want, wait a few minutes for a cloud to block the sun or for the sun to descend behind a hill. If you're photographing a person or other moveable subject, you might want to move the subject into the shade for soft lighting.

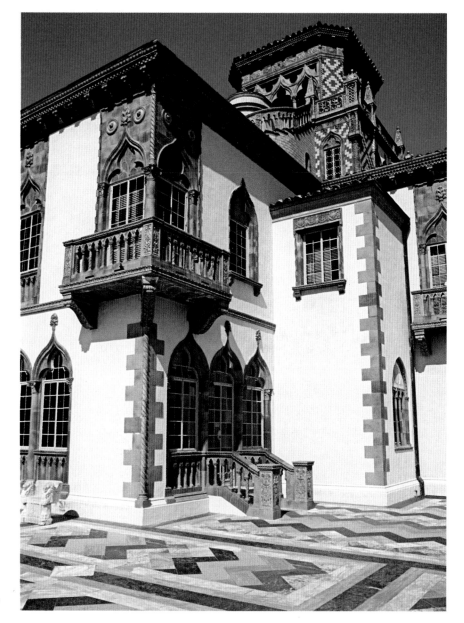

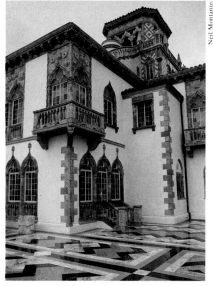

An overcast sky gives soft lighting with unobtrusive shadows and few pronounced highlights.

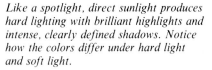

Like a spotlight, direct sunlight produces hard lighting with brilliant highlights and intense, clearly defined shadows. Notice how the colors differ under hard light and soft light.

65

Daylight film under fluorescent light

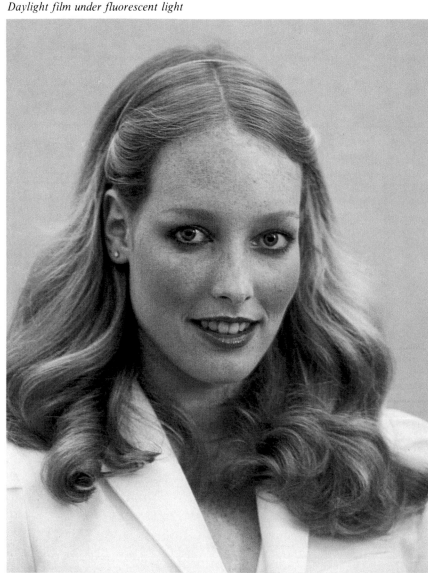

COLOR OF LIGHT

We tend to attribute color to the world around us rather than to the light illuminating it. The light itself appears colorless. But it isn't. The sun and most artificial light sources emit light composed of many colors. This is readily demonstrated by a prism splitting sunlight into a spectrum of colors or by nature's prism, the rainbow. Objects show color only when they do not reflect all the colors contained in light. An apple is red because it reflects only the red light striking it and absorbs the other colors of light. White objects reflect all the colors in light.

Although we do not readily perceive the differences, the sun and artificial lights differ in coloration. Fluorescent light is usually greenish. Tungsten light is yellowish. And daylight can vary from blue to white to orange. Our brain, however, adjusts to any slight color variation to provide us with constant color references. Thus, only a trained eye will discern a slight variation in color. Color film does not compensate for color variation. It readily picks up any color changes in light. Once you become aware of these variations, you can use or adjust for them in your pictures.

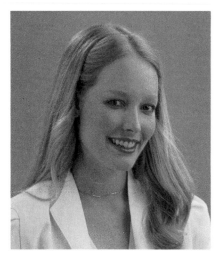

Daylight film under tungsten light

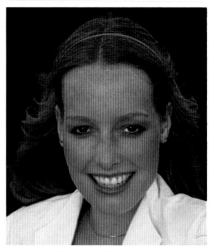

Daylight film under setting sun

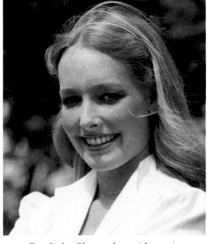

Daylight film under midmorning sun

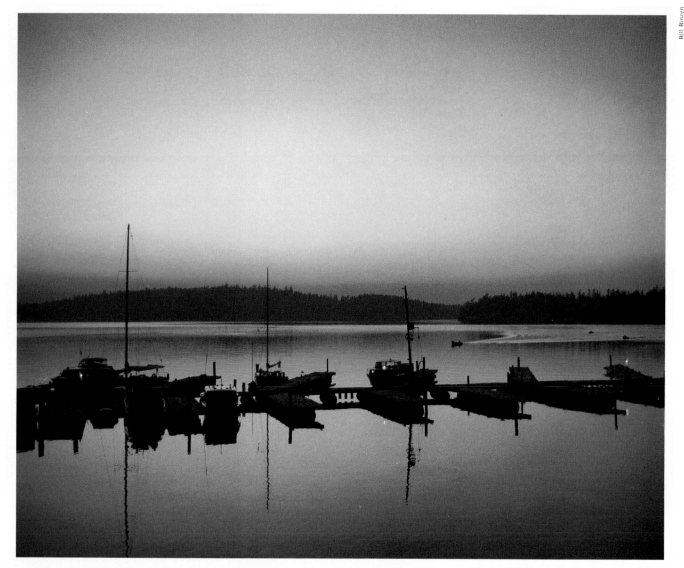

Bill Binzen

DAYLIGHT

About the only time daylight appears nearly colorless is at midday under sunny skies. Then the light is crisp and clear and shows things in strong, accurate colors. At all other times daylight shows some tinge of color. At sunrise and sunset, it floods the earth with warm hues of yellow and orange. At twilight, in open shade, and on overcast days, it carries a cool touch of blue.

Use these color variations within the light to create mood. The soft yellows and oranges herald an approaching sunset. They start in motion a whole set of feelings about the fleeting daylight. There may be fear of the impending darkness, awe of the natural beauty, relief and a sense of accomplishment for the day completed. Which feelings a photograph stirs depend in part upon the viewer's psyche and in part upon the subject photographed. A flock of birds darting through the twilight in search of a secure roost will not arouse the same feelings as a laughing face bathed in the warm glow of the setting sun.

The cool blues of an overcast day dampen spirits as effectively as the incessant drip from an eave spout. Through the scene and into the viewer steals the melancholy created by the soft, drab lighting. Without the cheerful clash between bright colors and shadows, the

A beautiful sunset instills a sense of peace and tranquility.

day seems subdued. It is characterized by a dim, uniform, and lifeless lighting.

With experience, you will learn how to use the color quality of light to reinforce your pictures. You can pick and choose times of the day deliberately to complement the mood you seek.

INDOOR LIGHTING

The most apparent differences between artificial light indoors and daylight outdoors are intensity and color. Indoor lighting is weaker than daylight. Unless you use high-speed films with ISO speeds in the 400 to 1000 range, exposure times will not permit handholding the camera.

Obvious to color film but not to your eye is the color difference between daylight and artificial light. To obtain normal coloration with tungsten lighting use a tungsten-balanced film such as KODAK EKTACHROME 160 Film (Tungsten). With tungsten lighting, daylight film gives pictures with an orange tinge. You can correct for this tinge by using a No. 80A filter with daylight film. It requires a 2-stop increase in exposure. With fluorescent lighting, daylight film usually gives a greenish tinge. Since there is no color film for fluorescent lighting, use a general-purpose fluorescent (FLD) filter or a CC30M KODAK Color Compensation filter with daylight film. Acceptable results are also produced with color negative films, such as KODACOLOR VR 400 or VR 1000, when used with either tungsten or fluorescent lights. Use exposure times of 1/60 second or longer with fluorescent lights. Underexposure may occur at faster shutter speeds because of the pulsing light output of fluorescent tubes.

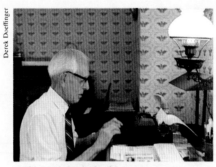

Unfiltered daylight film

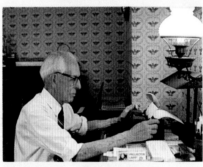

Daylight film with a No. 80A filter

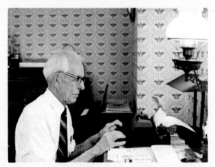

Tungsten light film

Tungsten-lighted scenes are best photographed with tungsten film, Daylight film can be used if you like the warm yellows it gives. Or you can use a No. 80A filter with daylight film for normal color rendition.

Without a filter, daylight film records most subjects lighted by fluorescent lights as greenish. An FLD filter or a CC30M filter restores more normal color rendition. A CC30M filter was used for the picture on the right.

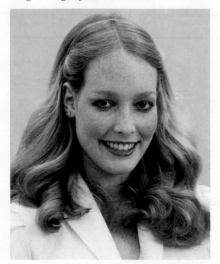
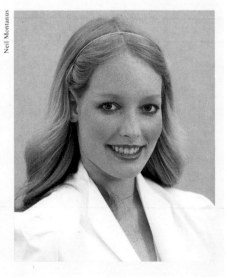

68

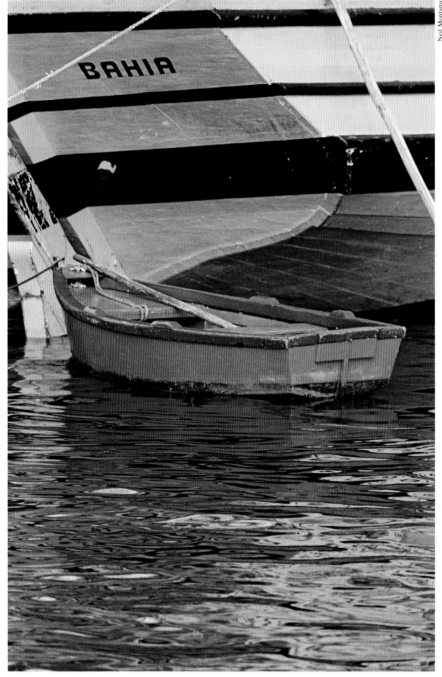

Neil Montanus

Sometimes the subject of a picture can be color itself.

COLOR

The eye revels in the sensory satisfaction provided by color. It also shudders when colors clash. Sometimes you may want to induce that shudder deliberately. Other times you may cause it unintentionally. You can manipulate your photographs through manipulation of color. Soft, muted colors found on a foggy day lend a quiet, pensive mood to a photograph. Bold, brash colors excite and stimulate. Colors influence mood both physiologically and psychologically. Intense reds have long been recognized as exciters, an association perhaps linked to the color of blood.

Color combinations are quieter when they are in harmony. Harmonic colors show similar hues such as green and lime or red and orange or even different brightnesses of the same hue such as pink and red. Colors seem edgy and restless when they contrast. Yellow and blue, green and magenta, these combinations seem to dance before your eyes. Include and exclude colors within the scene to match the purpose of the photograph. If you want to show color for color's sake, go ahead and do it.

Other than including or excluding particularly colored objects from the frame, your color controls are limited. You can wait for the color of light to change or you can use color filters. A color filter colors an entire scene with its own color. Intensely colored filters completely obscure most other colors, while paler filters let many other colors show through, although toned down. You can even use tungsten-balanced film outdoors for bluish colors or daylight film indoors for yellowish colors overall.

TEXTURE

Appeal to the viewer's eye through texture. Texture refers to the surface qualities of an object. Texture is most commonly thought of as smooth or rough, or somewhere in between. Best perceived by touch, texture normally pertains to relatively small areas appropriate to the size and reach of a hand. However, since photography records both large and small subjects on the same size film or paper, subjects of a grand scale can readily show texture in a photograph. A field of boulders or a chain of breaking waves shows texture in a photograph as easily as a tree trunk or a tortoise shell.

To stress rough texture, use sidelighting. Even an orange can be made to appear cobblestone rough. To suppress texture, use diffuse lighting or frontlighting. Either one minimizes surface irregularities.

By showing texture you tell something about the object. You help define what that object is. Moreover, you arouse several other senses and emotions that participate in and react to the perception of texture. The more you involve the viewer, the more likely that your photograph will succeed. Touch is the most obvious sense involved. It reaches beyond mere awareness of contact between a perceiver and an object. Associated with touch are the sensations of hot, cold, and pain. These are survival sensations and can stir strong responses. Touch also defines something as being hard or soft, dry or wet, dull or sharp. At the moment of contact your fingers quickly report much information. They tell you that a salamander is not only smooth but slippery, that cotton candy is not only gritty but sticky. Texture arouses many senses and feelings. Use it to engage, entertain, and stimulate the viewer's eye and intellect.

You can best stress texture by using sidelighting.

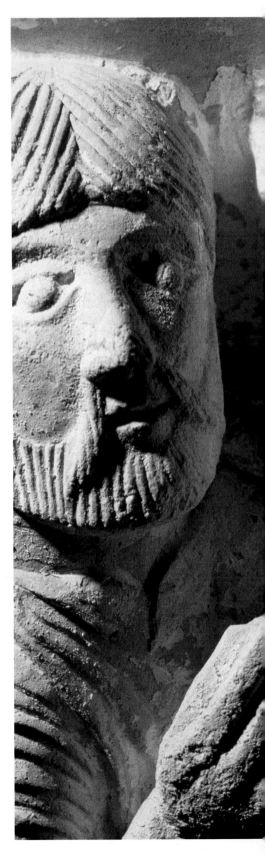

David Muench

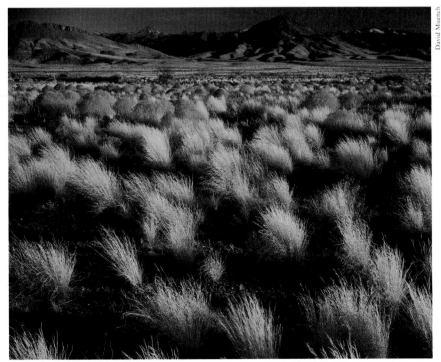

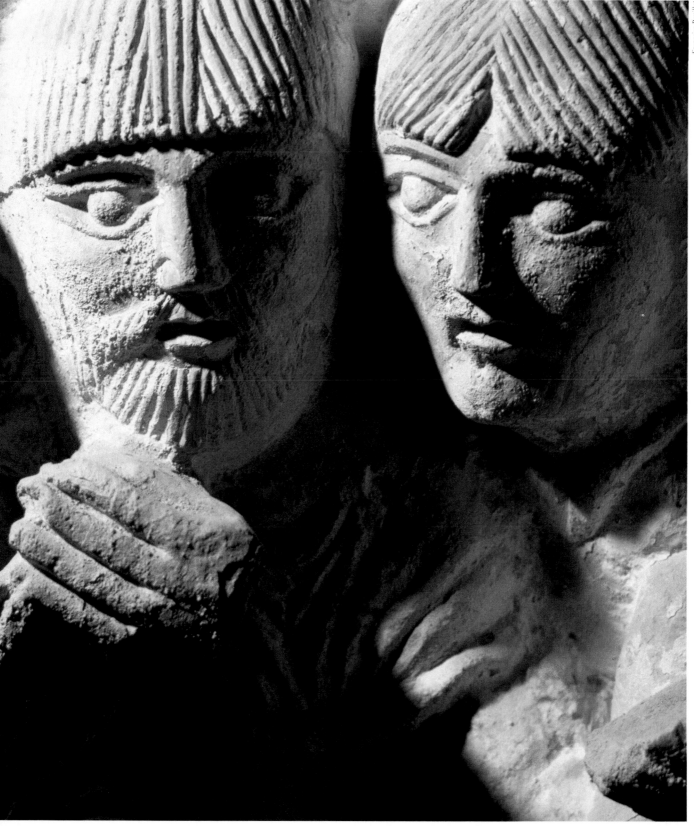

Composition

Composition refers to the arrangement of subjects in a picture. It is sometimes called visual organization or design. Composition determines the visual impact of the finished image. It requires careful deliberation, since you are not only setting the physical relationship between things but may also be trying to elicit an emotional response from the viewer. Following are suggestions that will help you make well-composed photographs.

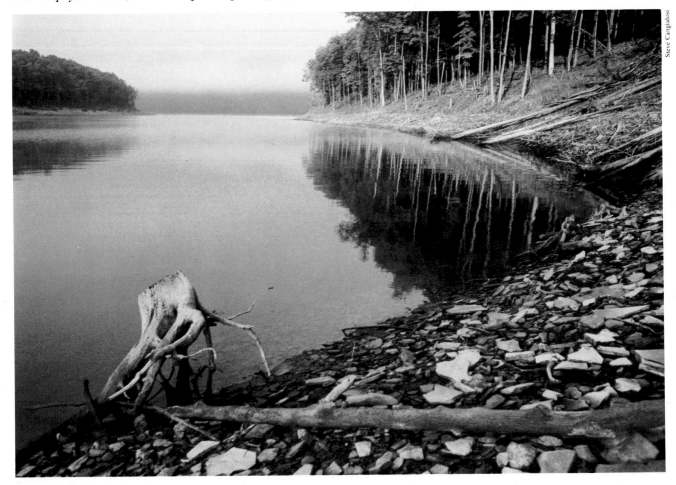

FRAME THE SUBJECT CAREFULLY

Think of the viewfinder of your camera as a picture frame waiting to be filled. Whatever you choose to include within the frame will be part of the finished picture. Anything you exclude from the frame cannot appear on film. Deciding what to include and what to exclude is a basic and vital decision in making a photograph.

Since most cameras make rectangular photographs, you'll also have to decide whether the picture frame will look better hung vertically or horizontally. Long, wide subjects such as a bridge usually look best framed horizontally. Tall subjects often look best framed vertically. Whenever you think this treatment inappropriate, don't use it. Do whatever is needed to make the subject look good.

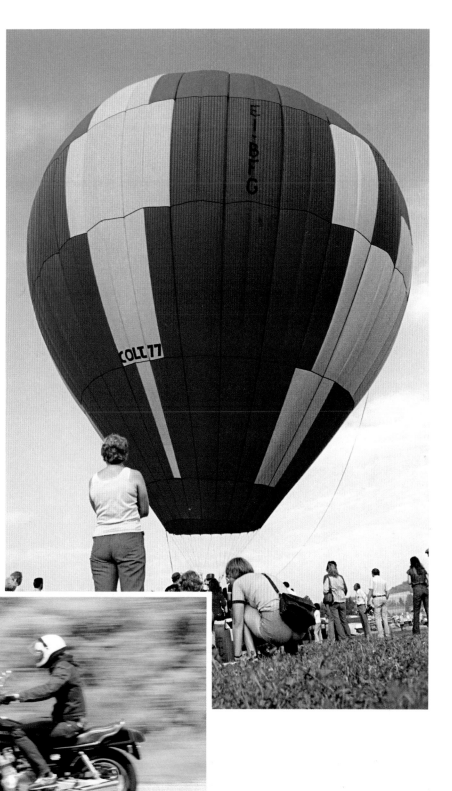

With a 35 mm camera, you can emphasize tall subjects by framing the scene vertically. You can stress wide or long subjects by framing them horizontally.

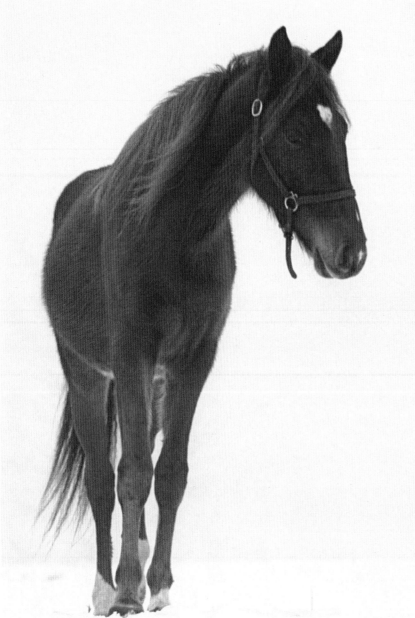

Robert Llewellyn

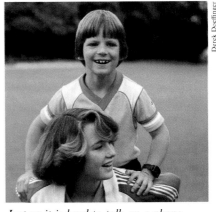

Derek Doeffinger

Just as it is hard to talk on a phone amidst the babble of a party so it is difficult to view a subject amidst the clutter of a busy background. Either move the subject in front of a plain background or use a large aperture to throw the background out of focus.

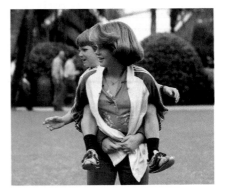

SIMPLIFY

A photograph should depict the subject clearly. A photograph should be clean looking, it should usually contain only a few elements, and it should be arranged in precise order. All too often a photograph is a welter of unrelated subjects clamoring for attention. In the end they all gain a share of the viewer's attention but dilute the impact of the picture. A good

Nearly isolated and nearly full frame, this subject is clearly depicted for you to admire or dislike.

photograph clearly offers one subject for examination.

Fill the Frame

An easy way to simplify a picture is to fill the frame with the subject. You can do so either by moving in close or by using a telephoto lens. Far too

many pictures suffer because the subject is rendered small and inconspicuous. It becomes yet another object in the scene. You may not be aware that you are diminishing the subject while taking the picture. Your eyes and mind tend to concentrate on the subject to the exclusion of all else. Your emotions may carry you away. Unfortunately they don't carry away the rest of the clutter and don't influence the camera's perception of the scene.

Shown big, a subject stands out. It poses in proud and glorious detail for all to see. Only people can be shy and retiring and still be appealing. Photographs have to stand up and present their messages clearly.

Sometimes you won't want to fill the frame with a single subject because you are trying to relate several subjects, such as a ramshackle farmhouse beneath a stormy sky or a long white horse in a shimmering meadow. You aren't featuring a lone subject but a relationship of colors and objects. Still you must simplify for the photograph to succeed. A white horse grazing on a green, treeless hill with a sliver of blue sky at the top is simple. It consists of only three things. But a white horse grazing on a randomly treed hill with a rusting tractor here, an abandoned wagon there, and roving kids everywhere is not so simple. When a picture has more than three or four elements, it becomes harder to handle. It can be handled, but make it easier for yourself by holding the picture elements to a minimum.

Although minimizing the number of elements and subjects in a picture often simplifies the task of composition, this photographer easily handled several elements through a well-chosen arrangement and viewpoint.

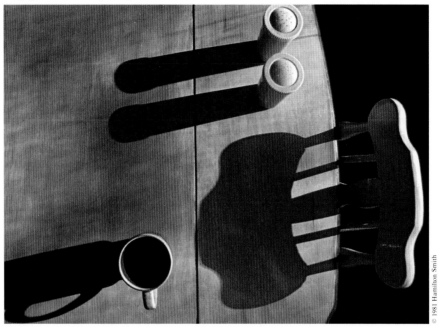

© 1981 Hamilton Smith

SILHOUETTES

Silhouettes produce the most dramatic simplification of all. Silhouettes strip away color, texture, and mass. Thousands of details are reduced to one element—shape. Only contours are left for the viewer to consider. In real life one is seldom forced to rely on contours alone. The eye and brain usually start with shape and quickly search for more information. With a silhouette a photograph can readily exclude all but shape. The eye leaps at silhouettes, devouring the sloping, curving, angling contours. The success of silhouettes may derive from their brevity. They show enough to tell the viewer what he's seeing but they hide enough to fire the imagination. Silhouettes are easily made by underexposing when the subject is backlighted or in front of a bright background such as a white wall or sun-reflecting water.

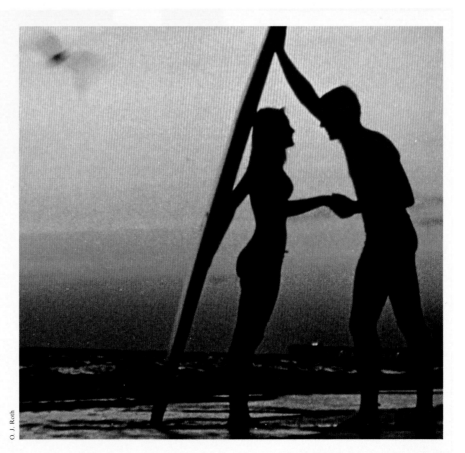

Perhaps the simplest of all pictures is the silhouette. Visual information is stripped down to the barest essential—shape.

O. J. Roth

VIEWPOINT

Since most cameras are designed to be used at eye level and since humans are upright creatures, most pictures are taken from eye level while the photographer is standing. There is nothing wrong with this. But it can become tiresome to see the same viewpoint used time after time. An abrupt departure from a standard angle can produce an arresting photograph.

Always look for better camera angles. They can turn a prosaic subject into a fascinating subject.

Vary your viewpoints. Supplement overall views with close-ups of details. Make a practice of taking several pictures from different distances and sites when confronted with a subject of unusual appeal. Often, the best picture develops gradually as you experiment with different points of view.

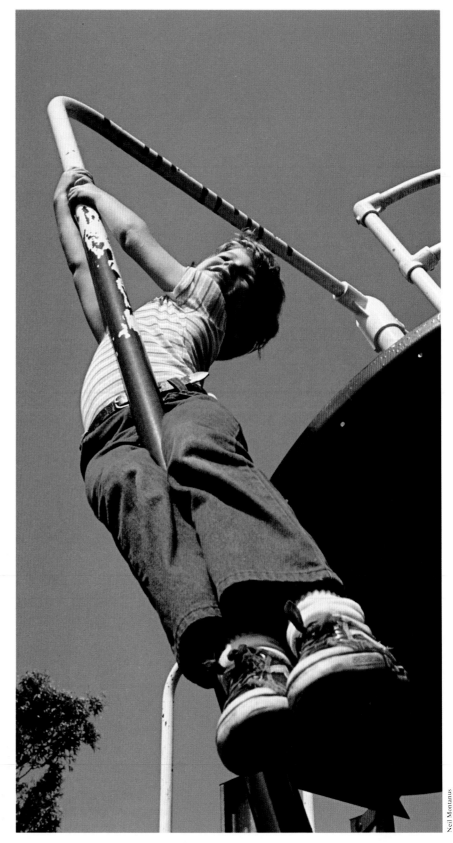

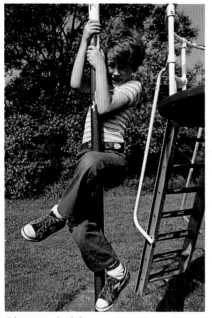

*Photographed from a normal, standing position, **above**, this child sliding down a pole looks pleasant enough, though quite prosaic. Photographed from the ground, **right**, the same child sliding down the same pole now appears dynamic. Viewpoint can make the difference.*

ASYMMETRY

Don't succumb to that seemingly irresistible draw that pulls the camera until the subject registers in the center of the frame. Move subjects away from the center. Left to languish in the center, many subjects seem dull and boring. They divide the picture area into regular portions. The right side receives no more emphasis than the left, the top no more than the bottom, Such regularity quickly dulls the viewer's eye.

By moving the subject off center you add pace and variety. You invite the eye to explore and wander about the photograph. The eye compares the weights given to various areas of the picture. It enjoys the variety of unequally divided spaces and, if satisfied that the results justify the treatment, will give its approval. If unsatisfied, it has nonetheless been momentarily entertained by the variety.

Normally, the subject will look best when moderately off center. Perhaps a third of the way up and to the right, or in the lower fourth of the picture. Yet don't ignore the possibility of extreme placement. Some subjects justify extremes.

SYMMETRY

Should you ever use the symmetry offered by placing the subject in the center of the picture? Of course. When? Why, when it works. That simplistic answer makes more sense than it seems to. There are no unbreakable rules of composition. What works often works in spite of any guidelines. So if the subject looks better in the center of the frame, place it there. Subjects that look better with central placement often show great symmetry. The central placement reinforces that symmetry and in fact makes the symmetry itself the subject, rather than the actual subject.

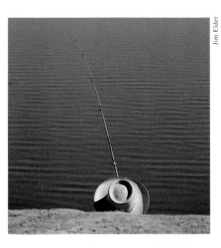

Jim Elder

Placing the subject off center often makes for a more interesting picture.

The symmetry of the balloons is reinforced by careful composition. Any far off-center placement in the picture would have unbalanced the picture.

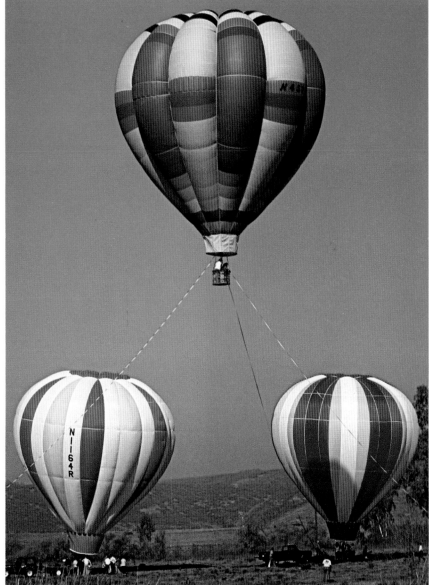

© 1981 Don Klumnn

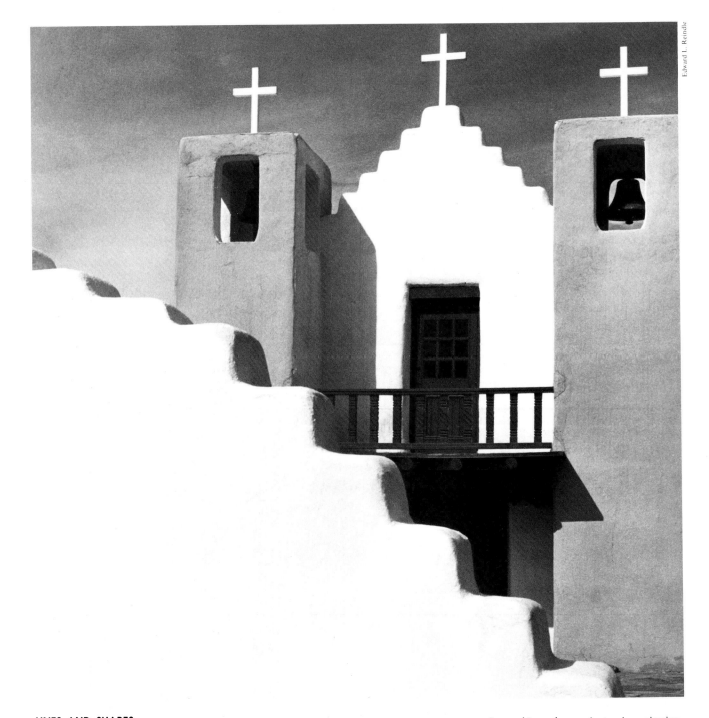

Edward L. Reindle

LINES AND SHAPES

Take advantage of strong lines, curves, shadows, and shapes in the scene. They let you take the viewer's eye on a controlled excursion through the photograph. A bold feature, such as a road leading toward the subject or a shaft of light picking the subject out of darker surroundings, provides an irresistible path for the eye. Look for such elements when you compose the picture. Put them to work for you.

Some things the eye just enjoys viewing. Strong lines and curves made by these walls and door are among those things. The eye is no doubt pleased by the order they present.

COUNTERBALANCE

Counterbalance occurs when you play off visual opposites against each other. Examples of counterbalance are light against dark, smooth against rough, angle against curve, colorful against drab. Opposites push and tug against each other.

While opposites may not attract each other, they do attract onlookers, in this case, the viewer. They create tension. Sometimes the tension is physiological, for instance, as the eye alternately tries to adjust for the black-and-white stripes of a zebra, or when fingers simultaneously feel both the smoothness and roughness of a marble in sand.

In counterbalancing opposites, each need not receive equal treatment. A black cat creeping below a white snowdrift can be shown taking up considerably less area than the snowdrift. The bright square of light of a mine shaft opening into daylight sufficiently counteracts a massive darkness that signals the interior of the shaft. In fact, greater emphasis is often given to a small counterbalance. It stands out by its smallness. The more equal treatment given the counterbalances, the less tension exists between them.

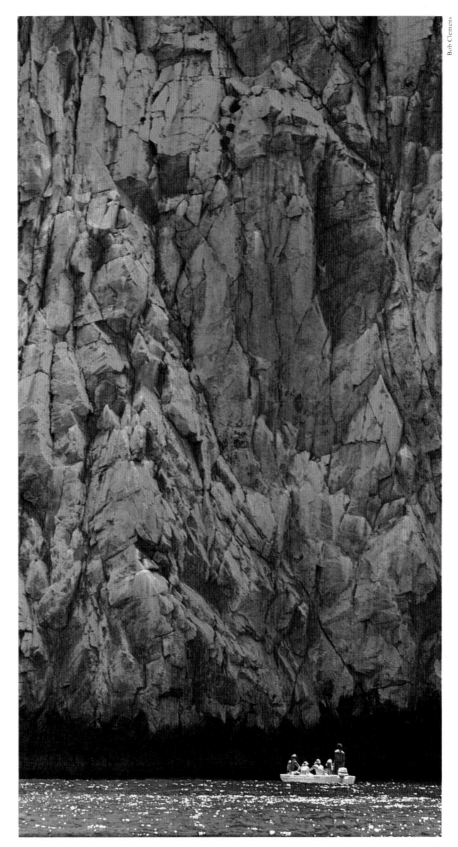

Several counterbalances work to make this picture. The cliff is massive. The boat is small. The cliff is shadowed. The boat is sunlit. The cliff is craggy and natural. The boat is smooth and manmade.

The subject

In the end, all you know about photography must be molded to a particular subject. Metering, camera handling, lighting, color, and composition must all meld together to showcase the subject. Yet different subjects require different approaches. A landscape may require sharpness; an action shot may not. A barn doesn't mind being stared at; a person does. We'll examine some techniques and ideas in photographing three favorite subjects: people, landscapes, and action.

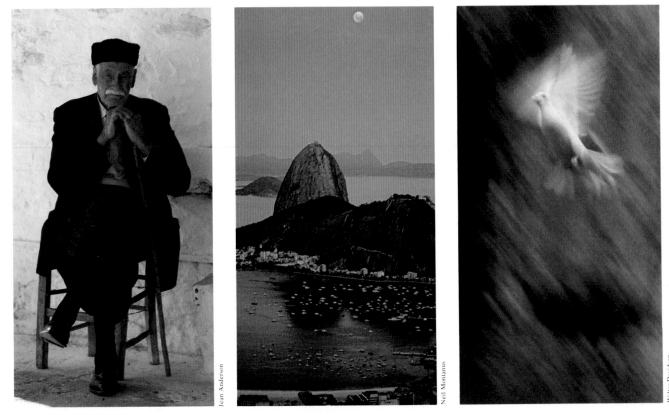

Jean Anderson

Neil Montanus

Walter Davidson

PEOPLE

Pictures of people invariably fall under two broad categories: portraits and candids. Portraits tend to be formal and posed. Candids tend to be informal and spontaneous.

Facial distortions appear in head-and-shoulder portraits unless a lens in the 80 to 135 mm range is used. A 50 mm lens can be used if the camera-to subject distance is increased by a few feet or if the subject tilts his or her head somewhat to the side.

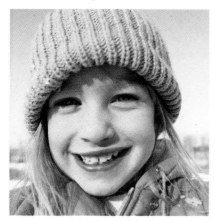

24 mm lens

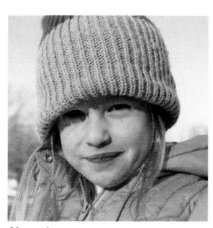

50 mm lens

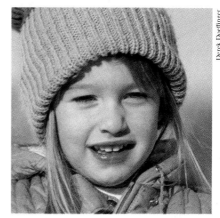

105 mm lens

Portraits

A good portrait reveals the nature of the subject. It may also tell us how the photographer feels about the subject. Pose, facial expressions, and props all can reveal the character of a person. Most portraits of individuals are tightly framed to direct the viewer's attention to the subject's face.

In a tightly framed portrait, have the subject gaze directly into the lens. That direct eye contact will engage the viewer. Focus carefully on the subject's eyes. If they look sharp, the pictures will be perceived as sharp.

When using a normal lens for portraiture, avoid filling the frame with your subject's face or distortion will result. The close shooting distance exaggerates perspective. It makes the nose disproportionately large when compared with the ears and other parts of the face. You can avoid this unpleasant effect by using a lens with a focal length in the 80 to 135 mm range. If you cannot use a longer lens, you can avoid distortion with a normal lens by keeping the camera-subject distance greater than 3 ft (1 m).

Soft, diffused lighting such as on an overcast day or in the shade is excellent for portraiture. It minimizes facial imperfections and doesn't cause squinting. With color transparency films, shooting under heavy overcast or cloud cover yields slides with a cool, bluish cast. For scenery and pictures of objects, the cool rendition simply maintains the feeling of the weather. The cast may be unpleasant, though, in pictures of people. To warm up skin tones in portraits, try a No. 81A or a No. 81B filter.

Forty-five-degree sidelighting can make a face look dynamic. Shadows indicate depth and size of facial features. A strong face is usually further strengthened by sidelighting. Use a reflector or fill-in flash to lighten any excessively dark shadows.

Since the face should dominate in a portrait, background clutter should either be avoided or rendered out of focus with a relatively large *f*-stop.

Eyes gazing directly from a photograph readily grab the viewer's attention as in this portrait of a Nepalese man.

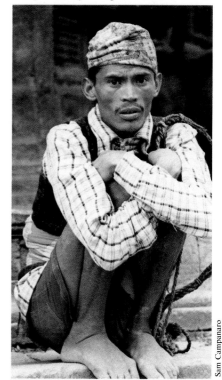

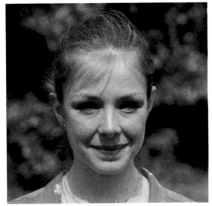

The harshness of frontlighting can wash out subtle facial tones and cause squinting.

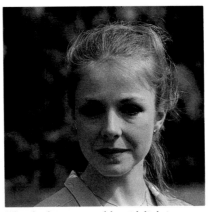

The shadows created by sidelighting round out the face and define the form of cheeks, nose, and lips. Shadows can be lightened with a white cardboard reflector.

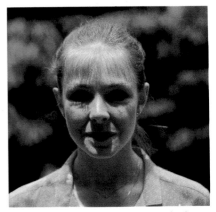

Toplighting causes unattractive shadows beneath the eyes and a drooping nose shadow. Again, a reflector can reduce the shadows.

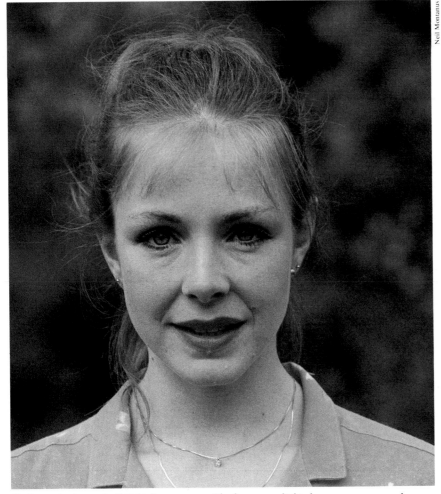

Neil Montanus

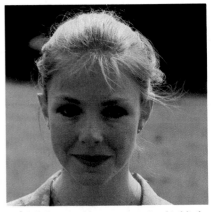

Backlighting adds an attractive highlight to the hair but can cause underexposure, as happened here. With backlighting the face is actually lit by diffuse skylight.

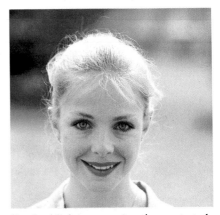

Perhaps the best of all light for portraiture is the soft, even light of an overcast day or of bounced flash.

Shadows are slight, hues are many, and the face is shown at its best.

For backlighting, opening the aperture 1 or 2 stops exposes the face properly but overexposes the background. Either minimize the background with a full-frame portrait or seek a darker background.

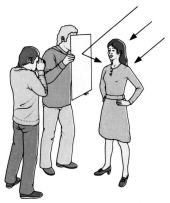

In this backlighted portrait, the photographer used a reflector to light up the face and avoid a burned out background.

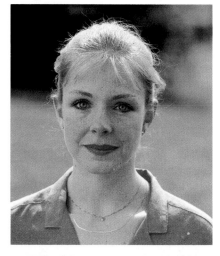

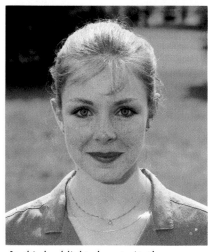

In this backlighted portrait, the photographer used fill-in flash to lighten facial shadows.

PORTRAITS OF COUPLES AND GROUPS

The relative positions of the subjects tell the story when making portraits of two or more people. A couple brushing shoulder to shoulder suggests more love than a couple 5 ft (1.5 m) apart. Eye contact is equally important. With small groups try for a triangular composition. By giving the group some form, you avoid sloppy composition. If there is a hierarchy to the group, the leader should be positioned prominently. From a purely practical standpoint, for large groups arrange taller persons in the back and shorter ones in front. Some groups might settle into a natural arrangement better than anything you can design. Give them a try before imposing your arrangement. Be sure to use a small enough aperture to provide a sharp picture of the entire group.

When you are using a flash unit for group portraiture be aware that direct flash falls off in brightness quite quickly. A group arranged front to back will be much brighter up front than in back. To avoid this, either use bounce flash, which is much more even, or arrange the group to minimize its depth.

Neil Montanus

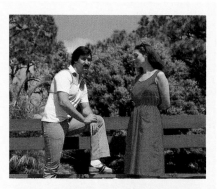

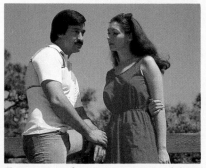

Eye contact, distance, posture, and facial expressions all contribute to the perception of the relationship between these two people.

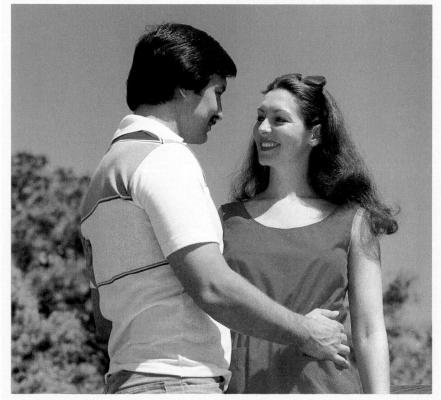

CANDIDS

Candid photographs depict spontaneity. They almost always show people doing something of their own choice, unlike portraits in which the subject is either posed or handling props arranged by the photographer. In a candid photograph the subject's actions give the viewer personal insight into that person and consequently insight into human nature in general. An adult slipping down a slide or a child soldering together a radio kit says quite a bit about the nature of that person. And its meaning comes from the person, not the photographer.

Though spontaneous, many candid photographs are carefully planned by the photographer. Assume that you spot a large puddle at a busy intersection. You can safely predict that patience will reward you with pictures of people leaping the puddle or leaping away from the spray of passing cars. Whether or not they avoid a soaking, you will be the beneficiary of their efforts.

An automatic camera is ideal for candid photography. It frees you of exposure worries to concentrate on the subject. Set the focus ahead of time. If possible, use a telephoto or a zoom telephoto lens so you can work unobtrusively from a distance. Once your subject becomes aware of you, self-consciousness might destroy any spontaneity.

For indoor photography use high-speed film such as KODACOLOR VR 1000. When possible, avoid flash. It can disrupt the naturalness of people and indoor lighting. Finally, be courteous. Don't take pictures of someone who doesn't want to be photographed.

The unguarded spontaneity of a candid photograph conveys a naturalness rarely found in portraits. A candid often tells us as much about ourselves as about the subject.

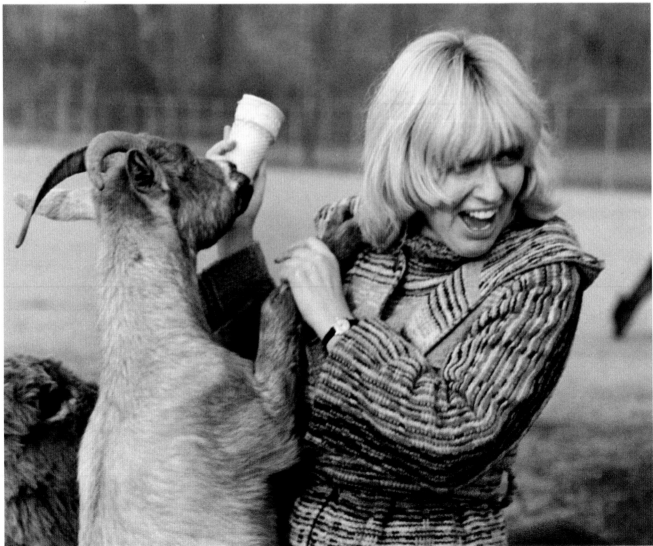

Derek Doeffinger

CHILDREN

Children are best photographed candidly. Although you can dress and groom a child neatly for a formal portrait, the resulting photograph seldom reveals the true character of the child. Few children would qualify for the best-dressed list.

Children differ from adults in two significant ways. They are smaller. They are more active. You can deal with the size factor easily enough. Simply kneel and shoot at eye level with the child. If you don't, you'll soon find yourself looking at a stack of pictures showing only the tops of heads.

Photographing active youngsters requires a few special techniques. If the child is dashing about in a playground or backyard, it may be impossible to focus as fast as the child moves. Instead of trying to follow the child, focus on one spot at a predetermined distance. Note several landmarks (a stone or a flower) that are roughly that distance from your camera. When the child passes near any of these landmarks begin taking pictures. Keep an eye on your shutter speed. A shutter speed of 1/125 second may work for hopscotch but not for hide and seek. Given the liveliness of kids, you can make your own life easier by using a high-speed film and taking along a flash unit, just in case.

To bring a child to a standstill, you need to engage and hold his or her attention. You might achieve your aim by starting a conversation or providing an interesting toy.

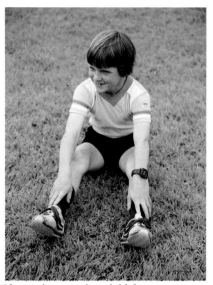

If you photograph a child from a standing position you'll either get a picture of the top of the child's head or the child's head awkwardly craned back looking up at you.

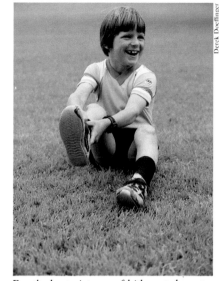

For the best pictures of kids, get down to the child's level where the viewpoint appears normal.

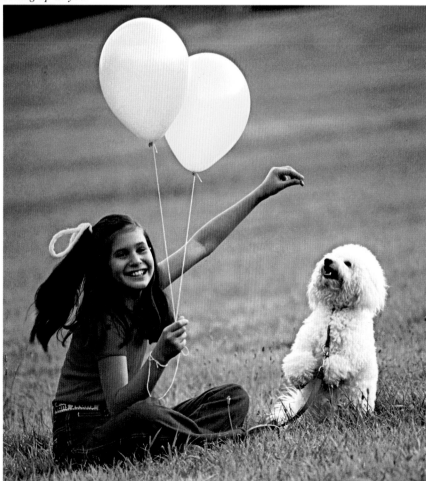

Full of charm and seldom inhibited, children have no trouble acting natural before a camera.

ACTION

There are two ways to record action: sharp and blurred. Each has its advantages. When a subject you are photographing moves during the exposure, its image moves on the film inside the camera. If the movement of the image is minimal, a sharp picture results; if the movement of the image is great, an unsharp picture results.

Other important factors to consider when photographing moving subjects include the direction of motion relative to the camera and the size of the image on film, which is a function of subject distance and lens focal length.

Shutter Speed

The most important single factor in controlling the way a moving image is recorded is the length of time the image is permitted to move on the film.

If offered by your camera, use the action or telephoto program so you can concentrate on getting the picture. To stop motion with aperture-priority cameras, choose a large aperture. The camera will automatically select one of the faster speeds possible. Check the depth of field and look for possible overexposure in bright light. With a shutter-priority automatic camera, set the shutter to the speed required to stop the motion. When in doubt as to that shutter speed, use the fastest speed possible.

Image Size on Film

Magnifying the image also magnifies its motion on film. It doesn't matter whether an increase in image size results from decreasing the camera-to-subject distance or from changing to a longer focal length lens. With a given lens, the closer you are to a moving subject, the faster the shutter speed you must use to record it sharply.

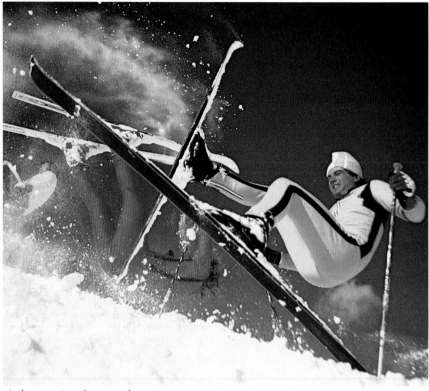

A sharp action shot reveals an instant in a rushing flow. Caught in midair tumble, these skiers momentarily show ballet gracefulness before ploughing into the snow. Shutter speed 1/1000 second.

To convey the sense of movement, the photographer created blur by panning the camera (see page 90). Shutter speed 1/30 second at f/5.6.

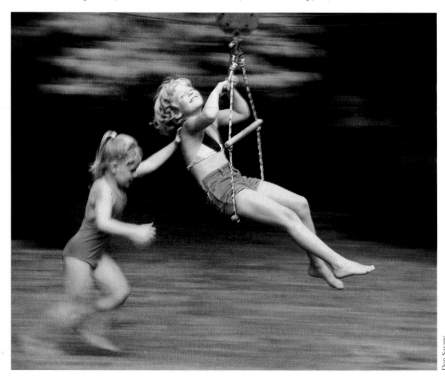

DIRECTION OF MOTION

When all else is constant, action-stopping shutter speeds vary with the direction of movement. The slowest action-stopping shutter speeds are for subjects moving directly toward or away from the camera. The fastest are for subjects crossing in front of the camera (parallel to the camera back). Shutter speeds in between the other two stop action of obliquely moving subjects.

A subject crossing directly in front of the camera requires a faster shutter speed to stop action than a subject moving in any other direction.

A relatively slow shutter speed can stop motion of a subject moving directly towards or away from the camera.

Stopping the motion of a subject moving obliquely requires a shutter speed intermediate to the speeds needed for the other two directions of subject movement.

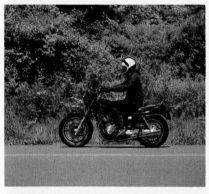

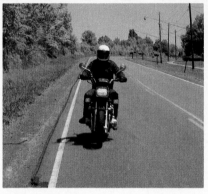

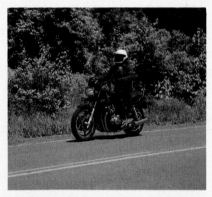

1/1000 second

1/60 second

1/500 second

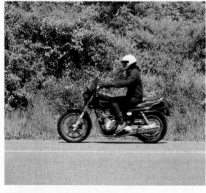

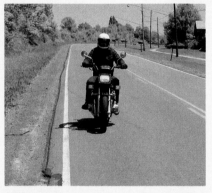

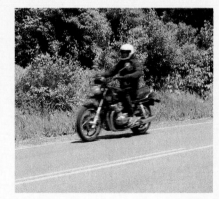

1/250 second

1/30 second

1/125 second

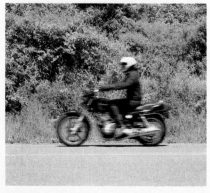

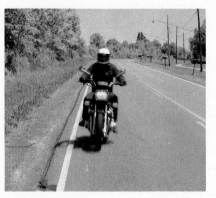

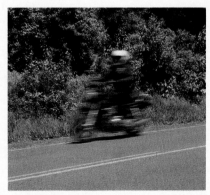

1/60 second

1/15 second

1/30 second

Neil Montanus

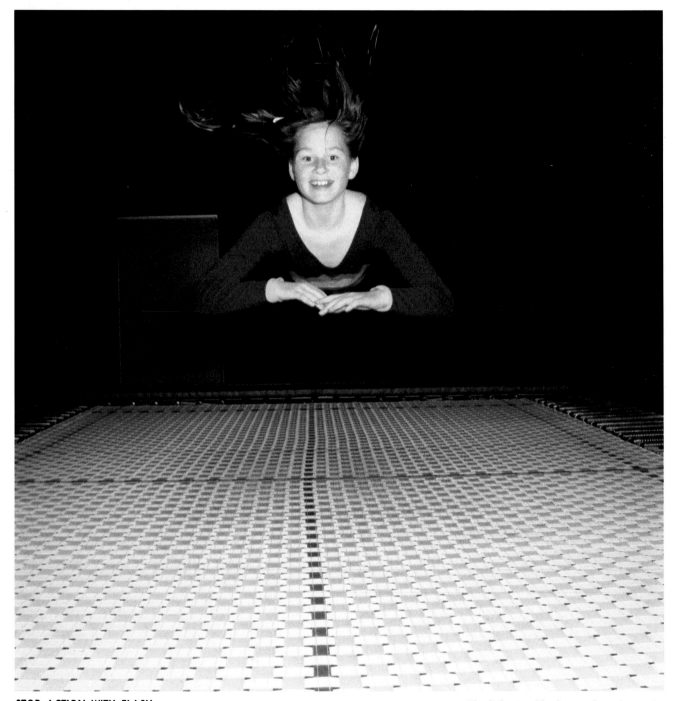

STOP ACTION WITH FLASH

The sharpest renditions of moving subjects are generally produced by electronic flash. The flash duration rather than the camera's shutter speed represents the exposure time. That duration can be extremely short. For small flash units, it typically lasts 1/1000 second or less. For some larger automatic flash units, the flash duration is as short as 1/50,000 second. As a courtesy, refrain from taking flash pictures when they might distract athletes, entertainers, or spectators.

The lightning-like burst of an electronic flash makes it ideal for stopping fast movement, such as this girl who seems to be levitating but is actually working out on a trampoline.

PEAK ACTION

Many subjects that have peak action can be photographed with fairly slow shutter speeds. The characteristic these subjects share is that at some point in their path they slow down appreciably before accelerating once more. The classic example is a diver springing into the air. The diver rises from the board rapidly at first, then reaches an apparently motionless peak before regaining speed in the descent to the water. When the diver is at the peak, a shutter speed as slow as 1/125 or even 1/60 second may give a sharp image. Even when stopping motion is not a problem, pictures made at a peak instant are often dramatic because of the feeling of anticipated acceleration. The peak does not have to represent an actual peak in a rising and falling path. It may simply be a slowing such as a running back reversing direction. The more you know about the type of action you are photographing, the easier it will be for you to foresee action peaks in time to take advantage of them.

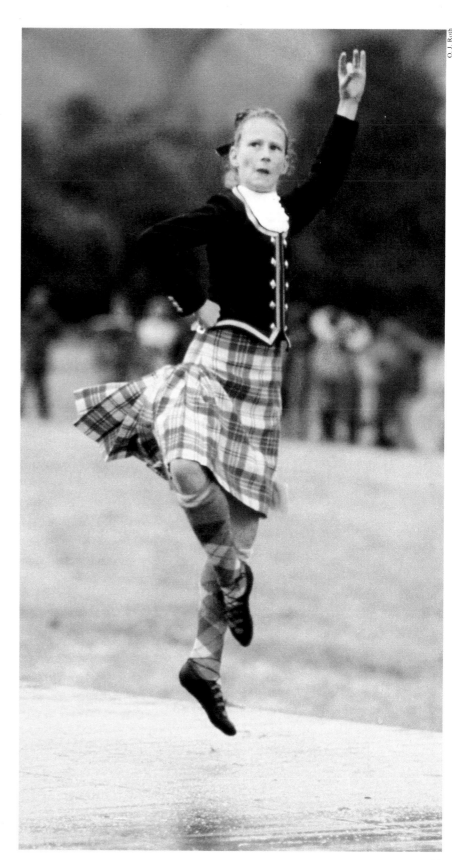

Many moving subjects reach a slowing or stopping point before accelerating again. At the point of slowdown, a fairly slow shutter speed of 1/60 or 1/125 second can often freeze motion.

DELIBERATE BLUR

Sometimes recording a moving subject sharply results in a picture that looks static, with no real feeling of motion. If everything in the scene looks sharp, you may have no way of telling that a race car was actually thundering along the track at nearly 150 miles (250 km) per hour. If you introduce a carefully controlled amount of blur into the picture, though, you can bring back some of the excitement the race car generated when you watched it. One of the best techniques for making exciting blurred-motion pictures is panning.

Panning

Panning consists of smoothly tracking a moving subject in the camera viewfinder while making an exposure at a slow shutter speed. This is one of the rare instances when camera movement during the exposure is desirable. For maximum effect, the subject should be crossing in front of you.

The resultant picture shows a sharp image of the moving subject against a blurred background. Here's how to do it.

Let's say you're at a harness race, with a clear view of a straightaway. The sulkies zoom past you from left to right. First, focus on a part of the track opposite your position where you expect a sulky to pass. When the sulky approaches, begin tracking it in the viewfinder. When it reaches the spot you focused on, press the shutter release, and continue moving the camera, maintaining a smooth follow-through. If you don't follow through, you might stop camera movement at the moment of picture-taking and lose the desired effect.

The slower the shutter speed, the more the background will streak, creating a sense of rapid movement. On the other hand, the longer the shutter is open, the greater the chance of recording the sulky less sharply than desired. There are no precise answers to

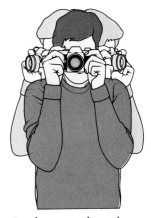

When panning, be sure to keep the camera moving and tracking the subject as you press the shutter release.

the question of which speed to try. Start out with a shutter speed fraction that approximates the reciprocal of the speed of the moving object in miles per hour (1/30 second for 30 mph). Use shutter speeds double and half this beginning speed. On bright days you will need a medium- or slow-speed film to obtain slow shutter speeds. You will also have to use very small apertures such as $f/16$. A neutral density or polarizing filter can help you obtain slow shutter speeds with faster films by blocking light without altering the color.

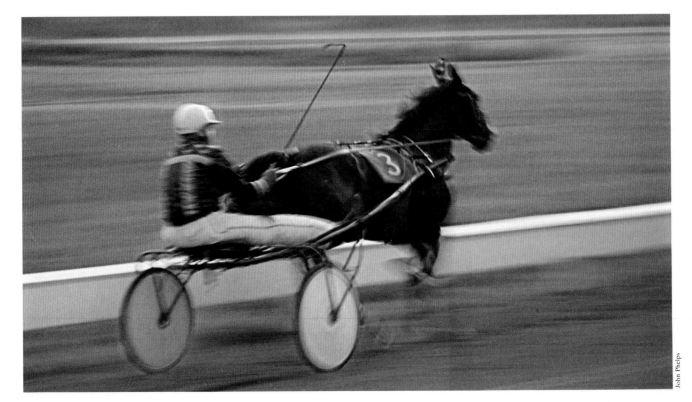

John Phelps

Blur: Camera Steady

An opposite approach to panning the camera is to keep the camera immobile on a tripod and make a relatively long exposure while the moving subject passes through the field of view. Depending on the speed of movement and the shutter speed, the subject may exhibit slight to pronounced blurring, while static parts of the scene register sharply.

Select a film with sensitivity appropriate to the anticipated light level. Or take along a neutral density filter to get slow shutter speeds. Besides obvious applications to sports subjects, allowing motion to blur during an extended exposure can produce subtle and lovely effects in pictures of natural subjects. The blur of motion softens breaking surf poetically and contrasts it with sharply rendered rocks or jetties. Leaves and grass moving in a breeze can become impressionistic masses of color in a landscape. As with panning, experiment to learn which shutter speeds to try first, and take several versions of each shot at a variety of shutter speeds.

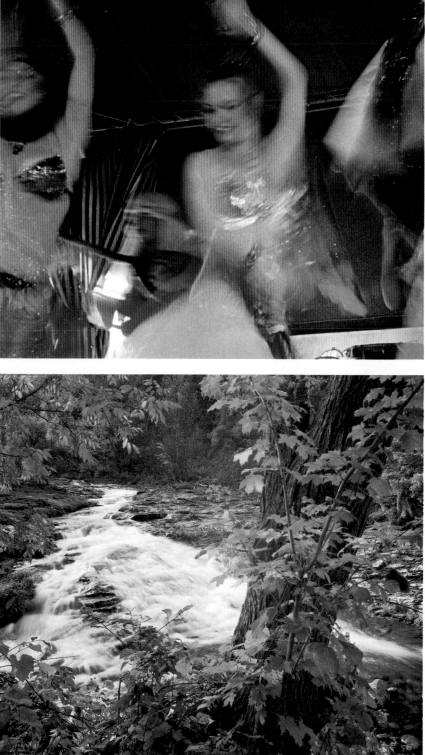

*By holding the camera steady and allowing the moving subject to create its own blur, **above**, you can produce startling images. The subject is portrayed in a way we do not normally see. Shutter speed 1/8 second.*

A slow shutter speed of 1/8 second turns the crystalline clear rivulets of a stream into a soft, white blur of water.

LANDSCAPES

To many people, landscape photography means capturing the breathtaking view from a roadside lookout or photographing that gorgeous chain of mountains against the deep blue sky. Landscape photography is that and more. It goes well beyond the postcard view of magnificent scenery. Instead of a rolling plain, it can be a crowded parking lot. Instead of a pastoral farm scene, it can be a jagged city skyline. It can be a flaming cloud at sunset, a shimmering reflection in the water, a wave crashing against a rock. It can be a moonrise, a smokestack, a cooling tower. Landscape photography ranges so widely that it affords many opportunities. Most of us choose to photograph natural beauty, but the other side of landscape photography is also valid.

There is a miraculous aspect to compressing miles of scenery onto the surface of a small piece of film. Nonetheless, resist the urge to cram the maximum amount of scenery into every picture. Reducing the horizon to the width of a frame of film diminishes the visual impact. Excessive miniaturization lessens the importance of key features. Concentrate on a significant segment of the scene. Show the subject clearly.

Although the configuration of a landscape may be relatively permanent, its appearance constantly changes. Time of day, time of year, the weather, and other factors affect a landscape's appearance. Weather and

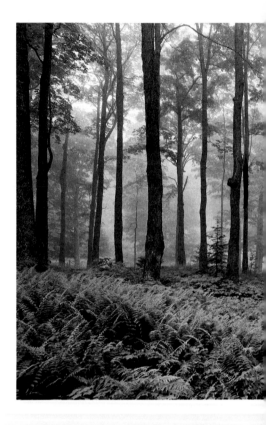

The most common landscape photographs are of pleasant pastoral scenes, such as this forest in the early morning mist.

HORIZON POSITION

Unless you are photographing a very symmetrical scene, the horizon should not cut across the center of the picture. A high horizon confines the viewer to the earth, leaving the eye to roam the land, symbolizing great distances to be traversed. With a low horizon, the earth and its structures are dwarfed by a great expanse of sky, suggesting spaciousness.

When placing the horizon low, be aware that the bright sky may lead the meter into underexposing the terrain. To show detail in the land, establish the exposure by aiming the camera slightly down to prevent the meter from reading an excessive amount of sky. Note the indicated exposure, then reframe the scene. Check the meter readouts again. If they differ substantially from the original reading, use the compensation exposure that will not make the sky too light or the ground too dark.

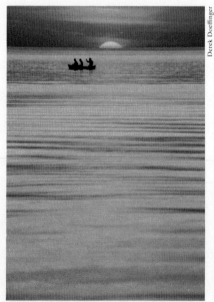

A high horizon directs attention to water. The eye travels from the ripples in the foreground to the canoe.

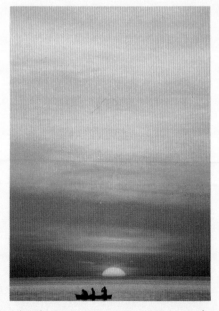

A low horizon suggests spaciousness and freedom. The sky dwarfs the canoe, showing how small it actually is. The viewer's eyes are freed to stare off into space, an action associated with daydreaming.

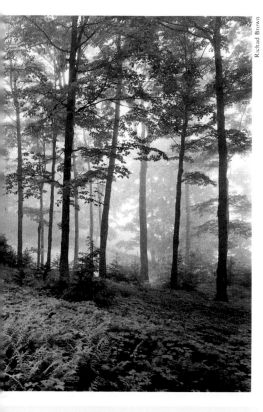

time of day may be the two factors you can most readily take advantage of. When seen under brilliant skies and then in a blizzard, the same landscape varies tremendously. By far, most people take landscape pictures under sunny skies, which allow them comfort and produce a scene as normally viewed. The resulting photograph is often satisfying in that it shows the scene clearly and is cheerful because almost everyone loves sunny weather.

Most landscape photographs do not require high shutter speeds, as there is little subject motion that must be stopped. However, extensive depth of field is often needed to yield sharpness from foreground to background. To obtain such sharpness, use a small aperture to maximize the depth of field.

You will often be using small aper-

tures to produce sharpness throughout the photograph. By using a slow- or medium-speed film you can reinforce that sharpness with a nearly grainless image. KODACHROME 25, KODACHROME 64, KODACOLOR VR-G 100, and PANATOMIC-X Films record scenics with superb clarity. Sometimes you may want the stability provided by a tripod. With a slow-speed film, small f-stops often mean slow shutter speeds. With a normal lens you may escape blur from camera movement at a slow shutter speed, but don't try it with a telephoto lens. With long lenses, mount the camera on a tripod. High-speed films also give good results and seldom require the use of a tripod.

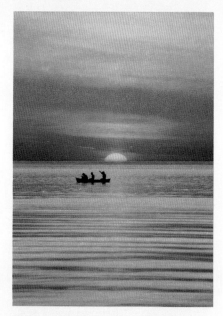

Placed across the middle, a horizon forces the viewer to look separately at the top and the bottom halves of the picture. An evenly divided pictures seldom works unless the subject is symmetrical.

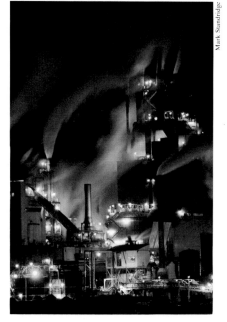

Glowing banners of smoke flowing from smokestacks and greenish lights and reflections lend an eerie beauty to an industrial complex. Photographed during the day, the same scene would undoubtedly be quite drab. With high-speed film or a tripod and an automatic camera, nighttime scenes are easily photographed.

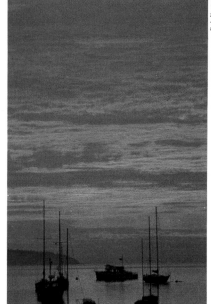

Landscape photography goes beyond the land. This brilliant sunset sky is also a "landscape." Reflections in the water, city skylines, and many other atypical landscapes are part of landscape photography.

WEATHER AND LANDSCAPE

Stormy weather inspires awe and fear. Who doesn't remember the blizzard of '76 or the wedding getaway in which the couple was pelted not with rice but hail? Use stormy weather in your landscape photography. Venture into a snowstorm or rain shower. Photograph the thunderheads looming over the horizon or the trees bending in the gale.

Even dull, overcast days can be useful. The nearly shadowless illumination that is so good for making pleasant pictures of people also can be used in landscapes. Under the soft, uniform lighting, colors look livelier. The absence of glaring highlights that dilute color and can wash it out altogether allows the film to record virtually all the color in the scene.

Since bad weather means dim light, you will probably want to take along some high-speed film or a tripod. KODACOLOR VR 400 and KODAK EKTACHROME 400 Films are good choices. You will also want to protect your camera from snow and rain. You can survive a drenching; your camera may not. Water is a deadly enemy of your camera's electronic circuitry.

Ideally, you and your camera will both function best if a cooperative friend or relative stands by with a big umbrella to shelter you. Such nobility of spirit being rare in the world, wear a wide-brimmed hat to help keep you and the camera reasonably dry. A lens shade is useful, even though there is no sun in sight, to keep stray raindrops or snowflakes away from the lens surface.

In heavy precipitation you can protect your camera by improvising a raincoat for it. Slip the camera into a large, clear plastic bag with the lens pointing toward the closed end. Use rubber bands to hold the end of the bag tightly around the lens shade. Carefully cut away the plastic stretched over the opening in the lens shade. Insert your hands through the open end of the bag to operate the camera.

In cold weather, if the temperature is 32°F (0°C) or below, keep your camera inside your coat when you are not taking pictures. The batteries lose power at low temperatures. Keeping the camera warm keeps the batteries warm and functioning.

Snow as well as sand is an efficient reflector of light. When taking pictures of snowy fields or sandy beaches, increase the recommended exposure by 1 or 2 stops. If you do not, the snow or sand will appear grayish, while other subjects are even more underexposed.

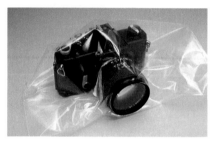

To protect your camera from rain or wet snow, place it in a plastic bag with the bottom cut out so the lens can poke through.

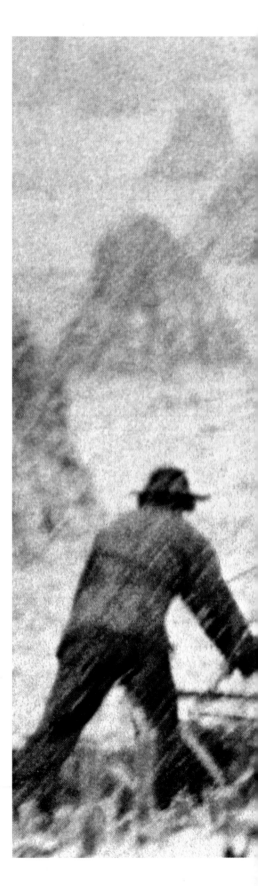

Driving snow and a man behind the plow combine to produce a powerful photograph of man against the elements. Bad-weather pictures often arouse strong feelings that involve the viewer in the photograph.

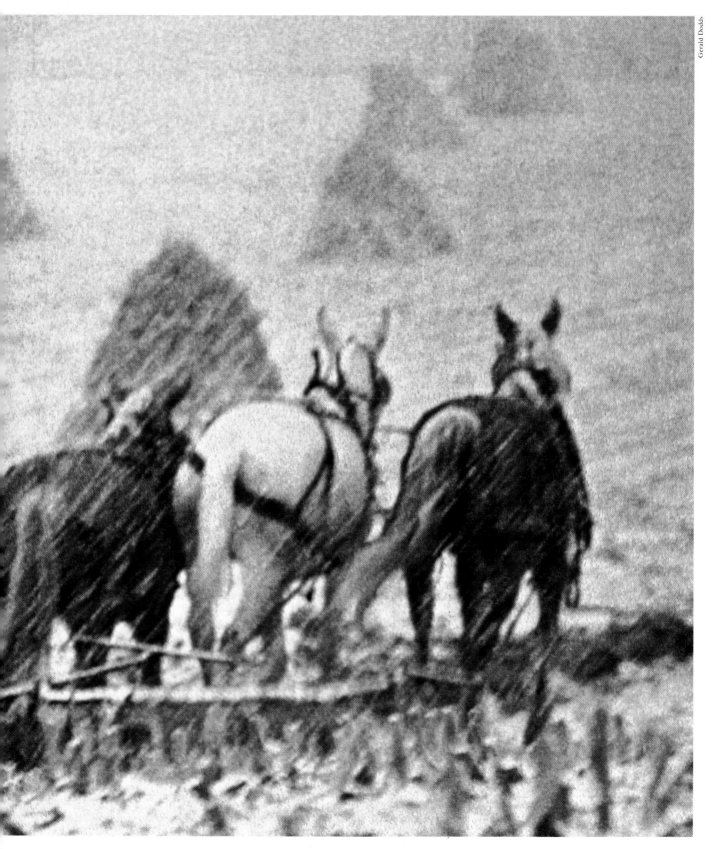

Gerald Dodds

Index